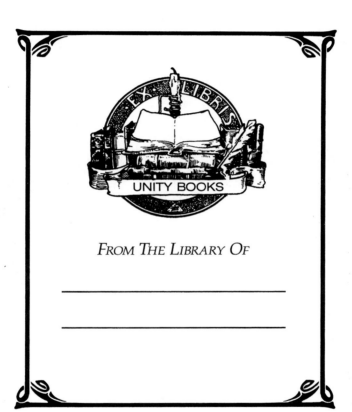

EFFECTUAL PRAYER

Also by Frances W. Foulks

All Things Made New (OP)
Myrtle Fillmore's Healing Letters

EFFECTUAL PRAYER

FRANCES W. FOULKS

Unity Classic Library

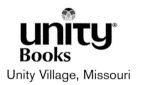

Books

Unity Village, Missouri

Effectual Prayer is a member of the Unity Classic Library.

The Unity Classic Library is guided by the belief of Unity cofounder Charles Fillmore that "whatever God has revealed to man in one age He will continue to reveal to him in all ages." The series projects Fillmore's vision of Unity as "a link in the great educational movement inaugurated by Jesus Christ" to help and teach humankind to use and prove eternal Truth.

To receive a catalog of all Unity publications or to place an order, call the Customer Service Department: 816-969-2069 or 1-800-669-0282. For information, address Unity Books, Publishers, Unity School of Christianity, 1901 NW Blue Parkway, Unity Village, MO 64065-0001.

Effectual Prayer was originally published by The Elizabeth Towne Company, Inc. in 1927. The first Unity Books edition appeared in 1945. In 1979 a revised edition was published. This, the third edition, is also revised.

First softcover edition 2011

Cover design by Karen Rizzo

Library of Congress Card Number: 00-100639
ISBN 978-0-87159-354-2
Canada BN 13252 9033 RT

"You have at some time greatly listened. Perhaps you were alone in the deep woods and the crack of a bough startled you, causing you to stop; and forgetting all else—what you were seeking or where you were going—you listened intent on finding out if there was an unknown presence near you. Perhaps you were one of a great audience, sitting spellbound under the words of some fluent speaker. . . . Or you were so entranced with the flutelike notes of some wonderful singer that you found yourself on the very edge of your seat. . . . Even more absorbed will be your attention, your listening, your stillness, even your alertness, when you have truly entered the silence and are waiting to hear the message from the Creator of your being."

—Frances W. Foulks

CONTENTS

FOREWORD

The cry of the disciples to the Master, "Lord, teach us to pray," is a cry uttered by each human heart, sometime, somewhere on the journey of life. It may come through physical suffering, through heartache, or through some failure to accomplish a great desire. It may come while one is undergoing great stress or strain or temptation, or when one is submerged in some personal grief or bereavement. Strange as it may seem, a great desire to enter into close communion with the Father rarely comes first through joy, during prosperity and success, youth and health; for at these times there is a certain sense of security when one seems sufficient unto oneself. We usually turn to God because of some need that we realize no human being can satisfy, and then truly our extremity becomes God's opportunity.

All of us travel the path from self to God by way of prayer. Little by little one learns to relax the physical so the God-life may enter; to let go the mental so that God-thoughts may take possession; to shut out sight and sound, emotion and desire, and become still before God. No one can take these steps for another any more than one can eat for another or sleep for another. Each one must take them for himself, at his own time, in his own way. Through many experiences we learn the way. Through forms and creeds, through prayers of many words, through desires and emotions the soul finally learns to cut out the unessential and go directly to the Father. Somewhere on the way each one learns to let go of self-sufficiency, through which have come his failures, and to take hold of the miracle-working power of Jehovah God, the victorious ally.

It may take months, years, ages, to become a righteous person whose prayers availeth much, but time is nothing to the soul who has truly set out to find the kingdom. Once the soul becomes aware of the divine plan and its part in completing it, the way is filled with victories, the path lighted by the angel presence going before to make plain the way. All trials and tribulations are swallowed up in the victories, forgotten in the joy of the knowledge that comes through achievement.

If the time of achievement seems long, pray. If the way seems dark, pray. If the results seem delayed, pray. Morning, noon and night, pray; pray without ceasing; pray in the night watches; pray and faint not; pray for those who despitefully use you; pray with the spirit and with the understanding also; pray rejoicing; be instant in prayer. Let praise and thanksgiving ever rise like sweet incense from the altar of prayer in your heart. Let the joy of inner communion open the way for you to the glory of God, no matter what the outer appearances may be. When this is done there is no force in the heavens or the earth that can keep your good from you; for you have become one with it and it one with you, inseparable, imperishable, eternal.

Beloved, while studying these signposts along the way to effectual prayer, may you feel the Spirit of Jehovah resting upon you. May you be given a "garland for ashes, the oil of joy for mourning, the garment of praise for the spirit of heaviness." May you in thanksgiving to the Giver of gifts, break the bread of life to many, preach the glad tidings, heal the sick, bind up the broken hearts, open the eyes of the blind, make the lame to leap, carry prosperity where before there was only poverty.

"Freely ye received, freely give": freely you have given, freely receive.

—Frances W. Foulks

"The effectual . . . prayer of a righteous man availeth much."

—James 5:16

The Meeting

And so I find it well to come
For deeper rest to this still room;
For here the habit of the soul
Feels less the outer world's control;
The strength of mutual purpose pleads
More earnestly our common needs;
And from the silence multiplied
By these still forms on either side,
The world that time and sense have known
Falls off and leaves us God alone.

—*Whittier*

Chapter I

EFFECTUAL PRAYER

MANY STUDENTS of Truth, when turning from the old manner of praying and seeking a greater knowledge of true prayer, make a great problem of entering the silence. Indeed the silence does seem a problem to those of us who have never assumed control of our thoughts, who have never learned the art of relaxation, of concentration, of meditation, of being still and listening within. These are all steps that are taken to enter the silence where God dwells and where we hear the "still small voice," with its words of wisdom and love, where we contact the gifts that through eternity have been waiting for us to become still enough and receptive enough to receive them.

The human race, at least that part of it which prays to God, has so long spent all the time allotted to prayer in beseeching a faraway God for material desires. Prayers have often been to a God who is nearsighted and perhaps a little deaf, immovable on His throne in a heaven, dealing out evil as well as good, and many times favoring the sinner in preference to the saint. People have talked *at* God, they have talked *about* God, in fact they have done all the talking, never giving the omniscient One a chance to speak back to them to assure them of His ability and willingness to give them even more than they ask.

The Psalmist said, "I will hear what God Jehovah will speak." We have the proof of his listening for and to God in the wonderful messages of the Psalms. The singing of those God-given songs restored the singer's soul, and they have led many other hungry, homesick souls back to the green pastures and beside the still waters, to "dwell in the house of Jehovah for ever." To the Psalmist, listening to Jehovah, God gave a long life full of rich living, a life physically rich, mentally rich. The experience of one human being can be the experience of all who are willing to pay the price. The price of such experiences as David's and Solomon's is to live the Christ life, one step in which is to learn to pray the prayer of faith that "availeth much in its working."

This prayer we do not pray, because we "ask amiss"; we desire the gifts more than we desire the Giver; we ask for things more often than we ask for a knowledge of the law and the strength and power to use it right. We have only to review some of our past prayers and their results, or even examine some of the prayers we are saying today, to realize that this is true.

All prayers are answered by the Father. Whenever a prayer remains unanswered in the manifest realm, we can be sure that somewhere there is a closed door between us and the Giver; for every prayer of every soul represents some need that, in its purified form, God is seeking to push forth into the manifest world. This loving One is ever seeking to manifest Himself through His children as health, joy, beauty, and wealth. We are the only means He has of coming into visible expression; and if each of us abandoned ourself fully to His will, the world would be again a Garden of Eden where we could walk and talk with God in sweet communion.

Each day we should seek to hasten this time by establishing in our heart the consciousness that He is all-knowing, all-powerful, ever-present, that He does hear and will give us the bread we crave instead of the stone that we manifest. Only those who become quiet and listen become still enough to hear the "still small voice" that gives this assurance. Such an assurance builds and strengthens faith, and it is only those who have faith in the ability and willingness of God to answer their prayers that are capable of receiving.

We build our own capacity to receive. Today we are building our capacity to receive the answer to tomorrow's prayers. Our capacity to receive is built by faith, vision, and expectancy; and the greatness of our faith, the height of our expectancy, and the steadfastness of our vision set the measure. A pint measure holds only a pint, no more; a gallon measure holds only a gallon, no more. Some hold out a pint measure to the Giver and receive according to their faith, their vision, their expectancy. Others hold out a gallon measure and receive accordingly.

There are many ways in which we limit our capacity to receive an answer to our prayers. Fear, doubt, and worry always close the inlet through which the answer would flow into visibility, for they carry us farther from the Giver instead of into His presence. The answer desired when the prayer is offered may never be manifested, for as long as we are seeking things, our desires change with the fashions, and there is no perfect pattern for substance to follow. Or the answer may be contorted and unrecognizable when it does come into manifestation because of a lack of faith and a wavering vision. Or only a portion may come into being, or the desire may become manifest in an unfinished and incomplete state, because our expectation has been limited.

Our answers may die at their birthing because there has not been incorporated in our consciousness the spiritual power and strength to bring them forth. Sometimes an intense desire voiced in prayer puts into action such a strong force that the desire prayed for comes into being before its time, is premature; we are not ready for it, and it entails great sorrow and suffering. Perhaps when the answer does come we find that we no longer desire it, have no use for it; and we may have to spend long, weary hours in prayer to erase the undesired thing from our life.

We do well to remember always before making our desires known to God that

> "The blessing of Jehovah, it maketh rich;
> And he addeth no sorrow therewith."

It is possible for our prayers to receive an answer in the twinkling of an eye, instantaneously, a glorified manifestation that is astounding, because we have asked with a faith that has given our desire into the will of the Highest. We may rest assured that under all conditions, irrespective of our seeming needs and desires, lasting good will come to us when we learn to ask that only God's good become manifest for us and through us. We can pray, "Not my will, but thine, be done," without the old-time fear when we remember the words of assurance from the lips of the Master, "Fear not, little flock; for it is your Father's good pleasure to give you the kingdom." When we come to the place in growth where we put the desire that God's will be done in our life before our personal desires, then the time is drawing near when all the good of the kingdom is at our command.

It is made very plain in the Holy Bible, which is the textbook and guide of all who are seeking to find God, that prayer is answered. Isaiah, communing with God in prayer, hears these assuring words, "Jehovah's hand is not shortened, that it cannot save; neither his ear heavy, that it cannot hear." Again he hears, "Then shalt thou call, and Jehovah will answer; thou shalt cry, and he will say, Here I am." Yet another time when he was listening for the "still small voice" these words came, "And it shall come to pass that, before they call, I will answer; and while they are yet speaking, I will hear." These promises are further confirmed by the One who best knew the Giver, "Your Father knoweth what things ye have need of, before ye ask him." To Jeremiah the inner voice conveyed the same assurance, "Call unto me, and I will answer thee, and show thee great things, and difficult, which thou knowest not."

The secret of effectual prayer is revealed over and over by the Master. He said, "God is spirit: and they that worship [pray to] him must worship [pray] in spirit and truth." To pray truly one must enter into the God consciousness, rise in mind to the plane of Spirit. If the prayers we offer are full of requests for things, we are in a consciousness of materiality and we are address-

ing our prayers to a false god that has no power
to answer them. Again Jesus tells us, "Except ye
turn, and become as little children, ye shall in no
wise enter into the kingdom of heaven," the
spiritual realm, from which all answers come.
Looking into the face of a little child trustfully
cuddled in His arms, Jesus once said, "To such
belongeth the kingdom of heaven." The heart
of a little child is pure, trusting, guileless, free
from criticism, doubt, fear, jealousy, covetous-
ness, hatred, and the materiality that fills the
hearts of most of the race as it leaves childhood
behind. Until we cleanse our heart of these errors
and seek to return to our original purity, we need
not expect the Christ to set up His kingdom in
our heart and let its good become manifest in
our life. "Ye cannot serve God and mammon."
The purest mind that ever functioned in a
human body received expression in these words,
"Blessed are the pure in heart: for they shall see
God."

When our vision is changed from material to
spiritual and we become pure enough to see the
good only, then we shall be knowing as God
knows and seeing as God sees, then will our
desire be "Thou only," and as regards the

heaven within, the kingdom of God, all things that we need and desire will be added. This is the fulfillment of the Master's promise, "If ye abide in me, and my words abide in you, ask whatsoever ye will, and it shall be done unto you." To this He added, "Herein is my Father glorified, that ye bear much fruit," showing us that it is the will of the Father that His glory be expressed through us and for us on this earth plane in abundant measure. "Much fruit" means all those things which are needed to make our life happy and beautiful and useful, devoid of anxious care, of hard work, of scrimping and saving for a rainy day. Let us remember in our prayers that the will of the Highest is always "good measure, pressed down, shaken together, running over," the "much fruit" of His promise.

Over and over we pray, "Thy kingdom come," and we, the only channel through which this kingdom can become manifest as a rose-blossom earth, accept the dearth and the famine, the weeds and the tares of a poverty-ridden world, and do not rise high enough in our prayers to wipe out this condition from our life! This condition will only change when we learn to

ask and receive as did the Way-Shower. He had
learned to pray the prayer of oneness with the
Father's will. He could say, "Father, I thank
thee that thou heardest me. And I knew that
thou hearest me always," and have instant
recognition and instant response to His need.
This One says to you and to me personally, "He
that believeth on me, the works that I do shall he
do also; and greater *works* than these shall he
do."

As you earnestly, confidently, expectantly seek
to become that righteous one whose prayer
availeth much in its workings, there will be
developed in you soul qualities that you have
never before known—fearlessness, patience,
compassion, self-control, discrimination, tolerance, understanding. As you keep the high
watch, as you associate with the risen Christ, as
you abide in the secret place of the Most High,
Isaiah's prophecy shall be fulfilled for you,

"Then shall thy light break forth as the morning
[wisdom], and thy healing shall spring forth
speedily [health]; and thy righteousness shall go
before thee [success]; the glory of Jehovah shall
be thy rearward [protection]."

O Thou Christ of the living God within me, reveal to me the Father, as Thou knowest the Father, that my faith may be strong, my vision high, my expectancy sure. Let all my desires and all my prayers conform to the will of the Highest, that my life may express only His glory, His beauty, His love.

Chapter II

PREPARATION

TRUE PRAYER IS communion with God, and our thoughts must take on the spiritual quality of God's thoughts if we would meet the great Giver face to face and receive of Him. The Master truly teaches this in His words, "It is easier for a camel to go through a needle's eye, than for a rich man [one immersed in material thought] to enter into the kingdom of God." Then to pray truly, a person must mentally unload his human desires and emotions, that he may become holy enough to feel the God presence, still enough to hear the God message, open enough to receive the God gifts.

In the case of every one of us, barriers stand in the way of our already answered prayers to pre-

vent their coming into manifestation, barriers
that we ourself have erected and daily maintain
in their solidity and impenetrability. Some of
these barriers we know—faults, habits, hurts—
but we have never come to the point where we
were quite willing to give them up, we have not
yet gathered spiritual strength and courage to
loose them and let them go from our mind and
life. Other barriers are more subtle, more deeply
established, unremembered. These are subconscious barriers, those of which the Master
spoke when He said, "This kind goeth not out
but by prayer and fasting"—that is, by cleansing
and renewing, by denial and affirmation, by letting go of self and touching the God-power.

Our life should be filled with good, because
everything was created good and given to us for
profit and enjoyment. When an error condition
in our life does not respond to prayer for its
removal, we have a right to ask why: "What is
there in me that is keeping this good from me?"
Self-scrutiny at times, if rightly entered into,
does no harm, but continued use of it creates
more error conditions like those which we see in
our search for the cause. When we do start to
seek out the cause of any error condition, any

unanswered prayer, we should first fill our mind with love and peace, build up faith, and enter into a realization of that glory which we had with the Father in the beginning, "before the world was." There need be no fear in this search if we let the Presence go before and lead the way, holding high the light that dissolves even as it searches out the error.

There need be no reaping of a harvest of suffering from this search if we remember that we continually have the ministrations of the Most High, ever ready and able to cleanse to the uttermost, lovingly cooperating with our every endeavor to let go of error and reach the higher ground of the Christ consciousness. As we put all in His hands we shall be filled with strength and faith, courage and poise, through the presence of the One, of whom Paul said, "We have not a high priest that cannot be touched with the feeling of our infirmities; but one that hath been in all points tempted like as *we are, yet* without sin."

If impersonal and unprejudiced and sincere search is made for the cause of an unanswered prayer for more life or love or wisdom or abundance, if we let no excuse, no self-pity, no blame of another enter, the cause of the inharmonious appearance will be found, whether we recognize it or not. The forgiving love of Jesus Christ, the love that said, "Father, forgive them; for they know not what they do," will wipe out all the errors of consciousness. The love that said, "Today shalt thou be with me in Paradise," will put in action the law of recreation, and appearances will begin to change, will instantly change, if our faith is strong and we are looking entirely to our Father, who is quick to give, quick to forgive.

Perhaps we shall discover that our eyes have been fixed on the demonstration of things; instead of trusting God momently for every need we have been going to Him only in our extremity, when human help failed and our own endeavors came to naught. Perhaps we have uttered selfish prayers, asking for those things which would deprive another, hurt another, not yet fully realizing that only the good that man spiritually earns can come to him. Perhaps we go to the Giver harboring thoughts of hatred or condemnation, forgetting the Master's admonition to become reconciled with our brother before approaching the altar. Perhaps we are seeking our own good, with envious thoughts of another's success and abundance; seeking freedom from debt, while yet holding another in the bondage of debt to us.

Few of us seek to enter the holy place without something in our heart that would profane the altar of the Lord. In this we are reenacting the sacrificial rites of the Israelites of old: we are offering polluted bread in our devotional. To us now, as at that time, Jehovah says, "I have no pleasure in you . . . neither will I accept an offering at your hand." Anything in the heart that is un-Christlike—hatred, criticism, intolerance, selfishness, condemnation, injustice, impatience, jealousy, even anxiety and fear—is like polluted bread and must be cast out before the Christ can take up His abode with us and do His perfect work in us.

If one person feels any ill will toward another, holds any unforgiveness in his heart, no matter how great seems the cause for offense, he should cleanse his heart with a "God bless you, I love you, and forgive you," and this blessing should be made part of the feeling nature before it is dropped. It may seem hard in the beginning. It may be only from the lips that the words come. There will come a time, however, if we earnestly desire to feel this forgiving love, when it will wipe out even the remembrance of an offense, and a great joy and a new freedom will take its place.

In the greatest of all prayers our Master said, "Forgive us our debts, as we also have forgiven our debtors." He also said, "Love your enemies"; and to Peter's query of how often he should forgive his brother, He replied, "Until seventy times seven," meaning until every offense was completely forgiven. Until we learn this manner of forgiving we need not expect much from our prayers, for we are lacking in that quality which is the fulfilling of the law, that magnetic quality which draws us to God and the good to us. The law cannot wipe out the results of our past errors when the heart does not contain that which is in itself the redeeming force in man; neither can the love of God enter an embittered heart, a hardened heart, an unforgiving heart and manifest itself in the only way it can, as health and joy, peace and abundance.

We need also to forgive ourself in the same way that we should forgive others. We may be condemning ourself for some past act that we call a mistake, and grief in the heart and a constant repeating of the act in the mind shut out the love of God, which has the power to make all things new. We should count each experience that has been ours as a lesson in the school of life, one through which we come to higher knowledge. It is only necessary for us to pass through an experience once, and we need not linger if we get the lesson quickly; but as long as we cling in our mind to a past experience it is given power to repeat itself in our life.

It is made easier to let go and forgive the errors of ourself or others when we remember that the forgiving love of Jesus Christ has already cleansed the whole world of sin—present, past, and future—and the manifestation of it in our life only awaits our acceptance of this and the living of a higher life. We need to remember also that in the mind of the Father there never has been and never will be any condemnation and that He who is most greatly sinned against recognizes it not at all. To pray without ceasing, that is, to look continually toward God and His sinless heaven, is to enter into this Mind which sees no error, therefore takes no offense and has nothing to forgive. Who are we that we should hug to our heart and pronounce an error that

which the Father sees not, shutting out our good
and the joy of life!

The quicker we take up forgiveness on the occasion of offense, knowing it is already forgiven,
the easier it will be and the less we shall have to
reap under the law. Did not the Master say,
"What *is that* to thee? follow thou me." Our
work is not to inquire into the failure of others to
live the Truth and, by recognizing and resisting
something that they have started in action, to do
time in reaping the consequences of broken law;
it is rather to give all our attention to ever
advancing toward the goal of our high calling in
Christ Jesus. Such an attitude not only makes life
more joyful for us, more productive of the good
for which we pray, but it adds to the high
consciousness of the race and brings nearer the
time when this forgiven offense will appear no
more in the hearts of men, when man and man,
nation and nation, will live without offending
one another. This constant attitude means the
accomplishment of our part in answering that
portion of the greatest of all prayers: "Thy
kingdom come. Thy will be done, as in heaven,
so on earth."

The preparation for prayer through cleansing

has a denial side, a tearing down of the old struc-
ture, preparatory to the building of the new, a
wiping out of error to make way for the entrance
of good. There is another side to the preparation
for prayer, that of affirmation or constructive
thinking, which carries us into the high watch,
where dwells the Lover, the Giver, the Knower.
We should never use any denial or cleansing
thought without immediately following it with a
high and holy aspiration or realization; for to
leave a vacancy such as a denial makes is to make
room for other errors to enter, and perhaps the
last state will be worse than the first.

There is a higher way of cleansing, when the
mind is ready to accept it, in which no denials
are necessary. If one can turn quickly enough to
God, refusing entrance to the mind of the error,
refusing recognition of it, and can keep the mind
full of prayer and affirmation of the good, the
error will be as effectually wiped out as is the impurity of a pool when a stream of pure water is
allowed to pass through it continuously.

We must conduct for ourself the search for the
closed door that is keeping our good from us,
keeping our prayers from being answered. When
the search is finished, no matter what is written

over the door, each will find that the real cause is
a lack of God in the heart and mind.

We have not often enough and long enough
lifted our eyes to the One who neither slumbers
nor sleeps, who keeps us from all evil; we have
not sought to dwell constantly in "the secret
place of the Most High"; we have not turned
often enough in times of pain to the Great Physician whose touch brings wholeness; nor in times
of lack to the omnipresent Banker who continually presses out substance into every receptacle
held out to Him; nor in times of darkness and ignorance of the way to the great Knower who
gives of His omniscience freely to all who put
their dependence in Him. We have not kept the
high watch but have let our vision drop to hap-
penings, seeing good and evil, and bringing into
our life the manifestation of this mixed state of
consciousness. We have called on God in another
consciousness than the God consciousness, our
mind more on the gifts than on the Giver. There
is something in our mind, before God, and we
are again the Israelites contending on Mount
Carmel and with the same results: "They . . .
called on the name of Baal from morning even
until noon, saying, O Baal, hear us. But there

was no voice, nor any that answered."

But when like Elijah we repair the altar within and in faith and purity of thought make our needs known, even though the waters of negation seem to surround us and overflow us, as surely as Elijah's God burned up the wood and licked up the water as a sign of His presence so will our God show Himself greater than any circumstance, greater than any condition or personality in our life.

To know God truly enough to receive is to know that He withholds no good thing from any of His creation, whether it be plant, animal, or man. Only in this knowledge can we ask, believing we have already received, and see with the God vision as already accomplished. He who created the "very good" still rests in this perfection and to enter this place with Him, if only for a moment, is to start into action something higher than the mortal knows. All that is less than good, all those things which bring sorrow and suffering, which leave regrets and bitterness, have been brought into our world through the wrong use of our power of choice. To acknowledge that we ourself have brought into our world everything less than good and to forgive ourself

for all the blame we have ever attached to God or
to others for the sorrows and sufferings that have
come to us are very important steps in preparation for prayer.

Do you believe this? Can you truly take all the
blame and give to the Father the praise and glory
for all the good of your life? When we know that
God is more willing to give the good gifts than
we are to receive them and that He is continually
pushing out the good to His children through
every avenue that they open to receive it, we
begin to assume the attitude of true prayer.

It is well always to have a fixed season and
place of prayer. God is omnipresent, we know,
but this habit of regularity seems to aid the
physical man to relax, the intellectual man to
concentrate, and let the spiritual man take full
possession. To go apart faithfully, earnestly,
joyously once, twice, three times a day as the
duties of the life permit and commune with the
Father, is the path to the attainment of the
Christ consciousness in which there is no separation of God and man in thought or manifestation. If Jesus Christ in His perfect conception of
oneness with the Father found it necessary to
withdraw from the sights and sounds of material-

ity that surged about Him and spend a time apart cleansing His human consciousness of these sights and sounds and renewing within Him the glory and power of His sonship, how much more should we do likewise, who have only in a very small degree entered into that perfect union. Just how much we need to leave materiality behind, to still the mortal thought and bodily emotions, to enter into the joy of the I AM, we do not realize until we practice it and come forth feeling that all things are made new.

If we make our time for prayer a holy time set apart for communion with our God and are faithful to it in mind, outer things in our life will cease to disturb us as we dedicate it to the Father. If guests are in the home, excuse yourself at the appointed time and go to the regular place, if only to say: "My Father, this time is holy unto Thee. Everything and everybody in my world works in harmony with Thy love." When this is done you can return and enter into the needs of the house with renewed strength, and enjoyment. If the telephone or the doorbell rings during the time of silence, let it ring a moment while you repeat your affirmation; then attend to it. No matter what the disturbance may be, do

not resist it or quarrel with it, or it will continue
to repeat itself. Bless the person or thing that
interrupts, seeing each in its right place.

When we really desire more than anything else
a period of silent communion with our Father
and appoint and dedicate a time for this purpose, the law by which true prayer is answered
will hold back every disturbing element, and the
mind of people who might otherwise turn to us
at this time will be given pleasant occupation
elsewhere. If some person continues to tread on
our sacred ground, we can operate in accord with
the law by using a thought for ourself and him
something like this one: Father, for myself and
(name) I ask that Thy power of love and justice
be now expressed in each of our lives. When we
pray such a prayer, the one who has been inter-
rupting will find some happy occupation at the
time we have set apart for worship, and this time
of renewal and communion will be left undisturbed. We have only to test God to prove His
promises, we have only to start Godward to find
the Father running to meet us, we have only to
let go of the self to find the greatness of His
presence.

Cleanse Thou me, O Spirit of love, from all conscious and subconscious transgressions of Thy law. Let me enter into Thy presence and see as Thou doth see. Let me bring forth Thy glory that the outer may become as the within. Where Thou dwellest in love and purity and peace let me there dwell also.

Chapter III

RELAXATION

THE MYSTICAL WAY of life everlasting in-
volves the body as well as the soul. In following
our old way of thinking we gave much attention
to prayer for the saving of the soul, but the body
received only desultory spiritual attention, and
that when it was under bondage to disease. Even
then there was little seeking or expectation of ob-
taining bodily healing through prayer; for the
prayer was usually "If it be Thy will, restore me
to health; if not, give me patience, make me
submissive." We did not realize that in God's
will for us there is only health and harmony and
joyful expression and that to be restored we have
but to enter into His presence and operate in accord with His will for us.

Each day we are getting farther away from the belief that sickness and death are the dispensation of the Almighty; we are coming to realize that these are due to our ignorant or willful transgression of the law of righteousness. We are coming into the deeper knowledge that the body is dependent on the mind for its perfection, that "man shall not live by bread alone, but by every word that proceedeth out of the mouth of God." In this knowledge we seek to open both mind and body to the word of God so that we may be filled with that which is productive of life everlasting here and now.

With this deeper understanding of the teachings of Jesus Christ and with the example of His ministry of healing before us, when we in need ask for complete bodily healing, we seek expectantly, and with faith in His presence and power we relax and rest in this trust. We seek to follow after Him in the spiritualization of our body, bringing it under the complete control of the mind of God in us, so that we may have mastery of it and direct it truly so as to serve Him and ourself. What pleasure is a body that is weak, suffering, limited in any way? Instead of keeping the body going according to our direction, performing the functions of life and enjoying its pleasures, we often humor it and coddle it and doctor it, sometimes giving our whole attention and time to nothing but its demands, and perhaps calling in the aid of others also. We are bound by such a body at the expense of every other interest in life.

Contrast with this the body that "goes and does," the body which to its owner is the temple of the living God, a body radiant, beautiful, vital, strong. A body like this can be the possession of any person who keeps his mind attuned to Spirit and his body open and receptive to what God-Mind contains.

"Know thyself" should be written large in our purpose and plan, and to know ourself we must deal with the whole man. One of the mysteries of the old religion was how God could be three persons in one. When we come to an understanding of our own threefold character as spirit, soul, and body, we shall better understand the threefold character of God as Father, Son, and Holy Spirit. The trinity of God, which is also mind, idea, manifestation, is continually in our mind, and when we are attuned to God, instead of relying on the limited ideas of our own in-

tellect, the Holy Spirit brings the Father's idea of
sonship into expression, to our good and to the
glory of our Creator.

When we thus know ourself as the threefold
creation of God and seek to keep mind, soul,
and body open and attuned to God, we shall
cease to be lopsided with sufferings in our
spiritual, mental, or physical nature, merely
because this side of us is closed to His thoughts,
His love, His life. We shall find the body obedient to, the soul eager for this teaching. We
shall find our emotions attaining peaceful expression under our control, and the ills that
through ignorance and lack of spiritual guidance
have befallen us, we shall find gradually fading
from our life. All the functions of our body and
all the activities of our life will again be controlled by the Spirit of God in us and find expression according to His perfect pattern for us.

To relax is to become open and receptive. The
body in its outer manifestation follows the mind.
Every ache or pain or diseased condition of the
body has back of it some inharmonious thought,
out of relation to the Creator, which tenses it and
closes it to the inflow of God-life. If we could
look within the little cells of the diseased part,

we should see each as a stagnant pool from which the pure, clear water had been closed off; we would see it all darkened as if its light had been turned off.

We have all seen persons in whom there was still the breath of life, but who looked like a house with all its windows darkened. We have also seen those who reminded us of a house set on a hill—they were illumined, so vital and living, filled with the divine essence of all life, open and receptive to the power of God in their body. Anyone who learns to relax and contact Spirit, who remains in this consciousness long enough will find the flesh losing its darkness, heaviness, impurity, coarseness, and the beauty and purity of Spirit will shine through.

A young person is more alive than an older one, because the former has not incorporated so many ideas of sickness and sorrow, limitation, poverty, and death in his consciousness to tense the body and disconnect it from its Source. The cells of his body are still connected with the energy or life of God that brought them into being. The Spirit is still able to function in the child, except at times when surrounding inharmonies fill the little mind with fear and tense the

body, shutting off the inflow. If in prayer we truly let go of the outer and enter into the God
presence, we become again as a little child and
receive of that which the Father holds for the
Son. In this attitude of mind we let the living
stream of life flow into every cell, purifying and
lighting it, giving to it its original state of perfection.

The more often we mentally enter in and lay
hold of the perfect pattern, the less attention
and consideration we shall need to give to the
material body. In this communion we shall
touch the mystical Christ body, and Christ will
give us to eat of His substance and drink of His
life. We shall build again a spiritual body im-
mune from disease, which will not suffer pain or
become weak and helpless. To commune with
this real body is to make the outer earth garment
like it. It was after such communion that the
Master was transfigured until even His clothing
glistened. It will be in some such way that we too
shall become transfigured, transformed, renewed. Then shall we glorify God in our body.

With a better understanding of our body we
come to that part of prayer which we call relaxation. In the last lesson on preparation we men-

tally let go of inharmonies, cleansing and forgiving. In this lesson we let go physically so that the mental purity that we contact in our prayer may enter into the flesh and perfect it. If the body is tensed and cramped, it is continually calling the mind away from its devotions. To be physically at rest in meditation aids in concentration, in cutting out the interference of the intellect so that the mind of God can function more clearly. Sitting in a comfortable chair with hands relaxed, at times with palms open in a receptive attitude, is a great physical aid to relaxation. If any part of the body seems tense, speak quietly but firmly to it in these words, *Relax, relax, relax, and rest in the Lord.* Speak as often as necessary to secure complete relaxation, pausing a moment between repetitions, expectantly listening within for the tenseness to give way and peace to enter. The body will teach us many truths concerning itself when we let go of the strife and strain of the without and go within to listen. At first the true message may be drowned out by emotion, pain, throbbings, or jerkings; but as we patiently and calmly speak peace to these, soothing them as we would a little child, always acknowledging the creative life within as doing the work, all in the temple of the living God will become quiet and ready for Him to express His beauty, His life, His being.

Those who are prone to live at high tension in home or business, who rush and strain to finish the duties of the day, who are of a nervous temperament will find that they become more and more receptive to spiritual strength, begin to walk more quietly through the day and rest more fully and peacefully at night, if they occasionally go through the whole body and speak words of relaxation to each part.

When they have learned to control the physical instead of allowing it to control them, they will find that it will cease to be such a problem to enter "the secret place of the Most High" and there find renewal of mind and body. When we are truly relaxed, we are as unconscious of the body as we are of well-fitting clothes. The body is the clothing of the soul and the soul is the clothing of the Spirit, and a body so cramped that it cannot let go and relax is closed to the beauty and life that Spirit seeks to express in it through the soul.

When your body begins to manifest inharmony, instead of fearing and visioning the outcome, instead of describing and enlarging upon the symptoms, you then should go apart, shutting both the door to the room and the door of the mind, and in quietness seek to still the body. Forget all the duties of the day, free yourself of all material things, and surrender yourself to God. The omnipresent life of God is all about His children, as free and abundant as the air you breathe. If you will lie flat and straight, and speak over and over words of relaxation to the body, especially to the part that is manifesting inharmony, and if you will rest in peace and quietness, in expectancy and faith, inviting definitely the omnipresent, omnipotent, omniscient Life to come in and take possession, then your body will be thrilled, filled, and healed.

What if it does take a few hours apart, or even a day and a night, to relax so that the God-life will have a place of entrance! Days of helplessness and suffering will be avoided, and harmony and refreshment and renewal will come that will increase joy and vitality as the days pass.

In learning to relax the body it is helpful many times to speak aloud the words of Truth that you seek to impress on it. Speak in quiet and peaceful, yet firm tones, expecting instant attention

and prompt obedience. Do not hurry. Rather be
lazy, letting the mind follow the words to the
part to which you are speaking, and stopping
there until relaxation is felt. Begin at the top of
the head and go through to the feet; then back
to the solar plexus (heart region, which is the
central station of the body) and there rest the
mind in some holy thought or appropriate
psalm. As one learns for oneself the correspondence between the different parts of the physical
body and the body of the Spirit, words will form
to fit the individual need and the physical body
will become open to receive and express its original and natural perfection. Until this time
comes, the following words will be found helpful
to relax the whole or certain parts of the body:

*"Look unto me, and be ye saved, all the ends
of the earth." Listen to the message that Spirit
speaks to the flesh, and listening, perceive and
obey. "Your redemption draweth nigh."*

*Scalp and hair, relax, relax, relax. Let the life
and beauty and glory of the Most High crown
you. I am overshadowed by the angel of His
presence, and there is continually being poured
out upon me a shower of blessings that far
exceed in number the hairs of my head. I am*

open to receive them in an ever-increasing measure of livingness.

Forehead, relax. You need not be tense and wrinkled from anxiety, worry, for I put my trust in the Lord. Thy name, O Father, written within my heart, sets a seal in my forehead that is my protection from all evil.

Eyes, relax. All the muscles and nerves in and around the eyes, relax, that physical weakness may pass and spiritual strength and life flow in. Mine eyes are ever toward the Lord, that I may behold the beauty of His countenance and the riches of His kingdom. Keep, O Lord, this lamp of my body single, that I may see only the good in persons, circumstances, and things, and that my whole body may be lighted with Thy glory.

Nose, relax, relax, relax. Let the Spirit of God in my nostrils make keen the discrimination that was given me in the Garden, that I may choose the good and leave the evil. "The breath of the Almighty giveth me life."

Mouth, relax, relax, relax. Let go of all error words that you may be an instrument through which the Beloved speaks.

"Set a watch, O Jehovah, before my mouth,
Keep the door of my lips."

Relax, all the muscles and nerves around the mouth, that the corners may turn up and outpicture the inner joy of the heart and the sweetness in the soul.

Ears, relax, that all spiritual deafness may pass from you, that you may hear the guiding and directing voice of Spirit. I am not rebellious about anything past or present. I am meek and lowly, willing and obedient, and my inner ear is attuned to catch the slightest message from the omniscient Guide.

Front brain, relax. I am not headstrong, therefore I do not suffer from splitting headaches. My human intellect is merged in the divine. When I lack wisdom I seek entrance to Thine omniscient mind, O Knower of all things, and Thou dost give to me liberally of Thy great knowledge and infinite understanding.

Base of the brain and spinal cord, relax, relax. Let the peace that passeth understanding flow through you and out from you into every center of the body. I establish Thy tree of life in the midst of the garden of my soul, O Jehovah, and its leaves wither not, neither does its fruit perish or decay. Its beauty shall be to me as an olive tree planted by the river of waters, and the freshness

*that comes from the river of life, flowing into my
soul, keeps me eternally young.*

*Vertebrae, relax. Relax to the strength center
at the small of my back. Let divine strength pour
through you into mind and body, making strong
all weak decisions, redeeming all weak sensa-
tions. Relax, vertebrae, to the elimination center
at the tip of the spine. Let me eliminate all error
from mind and body, let all inharmonies pass
into outer nothingness. Thy purity, O Spirit,
cleanses every physical weakness and makes
strong every vital part of my being. All old ac-
cumulations are eliminated from mind and
body, and I am eternally free.*

*Neck, relax, relax, relax. Be an open channel
through which the river of life may flow to and
fro, in perfect circulation throughout the garden
of God. Let me not in any way, at any time, be
stiff-necked, superior, proud, but let me be
poised and gracious in a consciousness of oneness
with all.*

*Throat, relax, that the power center in you
may be baptized from on high. All power is
given me in mind, body, and affairs through my
consciousness of the abiding presence of Christ
within my own soul.*

Shoulders, relax and let go of all responsibilities, that the great Burden Bearer may draw near and lift the load. Thou, O Christ, will sustain and uphold me, for Thy yoke is easy, Thy burden light. In Thee I trust and find surcease from labor, and rest to my soul.

Arms to the elbows, relax. Elbows to the wrists, relax. Wrists to the tips of the fingers, relax. In all that you do, do it as unto the Lord, and you shall be swift to do good and quick to execute righteousness. I am quiet, open, receptive, that I may be used by the Master, and that His law of giving and receiving may be fulfilled in me.

Chest, relax, expand. Lungs, relax, that the inspiration of the Almighty may fill you. Let me breathe in and breathe out the breath of God until I become a living soul.

Stomach, relax. The providing law of God my Father is active in me and for me, therefore I take no anxious thought, what I shall eat or what I shall drink. I agree with my food and it agrees with me. I drink of the life and eat the substance of the Christ body. I do not worry, I am not sensitive, I do not fear, but I rest in the bosom of the Father in peace and joy.

Liver, relax and let go of the bondage imposed on you by the criticism and condemnation of the human intellect. I do not judge according to appearances, but I do judge and am judged according to the judgment of the righteous One.

Abdomen, relax. Relax, all vital organs within your walls. Let the Great Physician have His perfect way in you. Let the Great Healer rectify all inharmonies. Let all physical waste be eliminated, let the waters of life cleanse you. Thou, O Father, who art rich in compassion and mercy, quicken Thy mercy and compassion through me and toward me.

Generative organs, relax. All the thoughts of my mind and the desires of my life are lifted up through the consciousness of the indwelling Christ; and the river of life, flowing freely through me, cleanses and renews every atom of my being. I thank Thee, O God, for the regenerating, purifying process now taking place in me, making me a new creature through and through.

Hips, relax. You are not weighted down by the burdens of the body, neither am I weighted down by the cares of life. Through the realization of the presence of Christ I am eternally young and free.

Thighs to the knees, relax. Thou, O Father, hath made firm the weak knees.

Knees to the ankles, relax. I am continually upheld, because I know that underneath are the everlasting arms.

Ankles to the tips of the toes, relax. I walk quietly before the Lord, therefore I am strong. The oil of divine love lubricates all the joints of my body, dissolves all hardness and harmonizes mind and body so that they can express themselves according to the perfect pattern.

Feet, relax, that you may not slip from the path of perfect expression. My understanding is now at one with Divine Mind. Because, O Christ, Thou hast plucked my feet out of a net and set them on a rock, and established my going, I mount up with wings as the eagle, I run and am never weary, I walk and faint not.

Heart, relax, that there may be wiped from you all bitterness, all hardness, all hatred, through the forgiving love of Christ Jesus. Love never faileth, neither do you fail in any of your functions. God is the strength of my heart and each cell in my heart partakes of this strength. I have set up Thy throne in my heart, O King of my life, and my flesh rests in hope. My heart continually rejoices, because I am at peace with all mankind.

Solar plexus, sun of my soul, light of my body, shine out the glory of thy Creator into every part of my being, that I may be restored to the perfect image and likeness, to the pattern in the mount, my eternal birthright and heritage from my Father.

Here at this center, this central station, rest until all the words have become flesh and dwell in the different parts of the body to which they have been spoken. Give thanks to God. Let the inner song of praise that the soul knows find its way into the thoughts, and hold your vision to the high watch as the daily duties are again taken up.

When the body has become obedient to the thought and the thought has become obedient to the Spirit, a "Holy Trinity" will be established, a constant inner glory that will be a halo of protection, satisfying soul and body with its sustaining substance. Then will accident cease to mar the body, disease to rack it, death to claim it. Through the body's obedience to the Christ Mind within, it will become strong, supple, immortal, the body radiant, a fit dwelling place for

the Spirit of God, and a beautiful expression of
the mystical, Christ body.

*My Father, my Creator, Thou whose likeness I
am, whose image I bear, let my mind compre-
hend Thy beauty and purity, my body radiate it,
my life express it to Thy glory. May I let go of
every thought, every desire, every material
possession that hinders this perfection from
becoming my own. I am open and receptive to
the river of Thy cleansing and renewing, and it
flows through and through me, making me a
new creature in Christ Jesus, every whit whole.*

Chapter IV

CONCENTRATION

IN THE JOURNEY out from God we have all become Adam-minded; that is, our consciousness has contained both good and evil, and we have entertained as true the thoughts that have built such a consciousness. Even after we have come to ourself in a country afar and have said, "I will arise and go to my father," and after we have truly arisen and started on the journey back, we have to be infinitely patient with ourself.

The old thoughts have a way sometimes of surprising us when we think we are fairly done with them, and they seem to push themselves forward in our mind as if to say, "Worship me." There seems to be no time when this is truer than when

we seek to enter the holy of holies. We then find
these irrelevant thoughts trying to bombard us.
At this time we find many thoughts that need redeeming and lifting up, which can come about
only through our concentrating on high and holy
thoughts, giving them constant attention, holding them close in the heart and letting our words
take form from them, our acts pattern after
them. Thus we shall be brought to a consciousness of freedom from Adam's duality.

In the old Adam state of mind we filled our
consciousness with a mass of unlovely thoughts
that created conditions like themselves in our
body and affairs. We have concentrated, whether we call it this or not, on thoughts of lack,
limitation, accident, sickness, and death. We
have feared, we have doubted, we have let our
mind be shaken with emotion—all the result of
concentration, for concentration is nothing more
than fixing the attention of the mind on one
thing. We have only to think for a moment to
realize that our subconscious holds a con-
glomerate thought mass, all built in by none but
our own self, and that it must be torn down and
rebuilt by this same self.

In only one way can the conditions be broken

up and dissolved so that they can produce no more, and that is by lifting up our human mind and merging it with the Christ Mind. This is accomplished through our holding fast to holy thoughts. We are to let go of the Adam thoughts and take hold of the Christ thoughts, as Paul says, "Have this mind in you, which was also in Christ Jesus."

Concentration on one kind of thoughts, error thoughts, has built up a consciousness of error, and these error thoughts have been reproduced in the life as error conditions. Emptying ourself of these and concentrating on higher thoughts will lift our mind into the Christ consciousness, and this in turn will be reproduced as harmony in body and affairs. First the within, then the without; first the sowing, then the reaping. There is no other way.

Our mind is one, but is active on three levels: that of the superconscious or Christ Mind in us, in which all spiritual thoughts originate; that of the conscious or human mind, which forms its opinions and chooses its line of action either from the superconscious or from outer appearances and personalities; and that of the subconscious mind or mental storehouse, in which is filed away all the thoughts of the conscious mind and which seeks at some time to reproduce in the outer these thoughts which we have given it. Thus we see the importance of turning the attention of the conscious mind to the superconscious and keeping it there so that the subconscious may be given good material and right instruction with which to work out perfect manifestations in the life.

If there is an appearance of sickness, poverty or an inharmonious environment in our life, it is useless to turn without to seek the cause. It is useless to blame people or conditions. It is useless to pray to God to remove the appearance, for to pray truly we must seek to rid ourself of the cause of unhappiness. God will help us to do this, and a new within will bring a changed without.

Our consciousness is built up by the thoughts that the conscious mind has poured into the subconscious since Spirit gave it birth and the power of choice. This does not mean one life but many, and there are stored away many sickness, poverty, and inharmony thoughts in the soul. Our soul knows of our birthright, our sonship, and when we begin to agree with the soul and begin to claim our inheritance, the errors are pushed out. For this reason when seeking to change an outer condition we take spiritual thoughts that relate to the condition we desire to change, so that these may be built into the soul in place of the old thoughts. We concentrate on these holy thoughts and build them strong within. These new thoughts which we use should not come from the intellect but from the superconscious or Christ Mind.

If we have not reached the point at which we can receive these direct, they will be given us through some person who has become one with Omniscience. Perhaps a book comes into our hands that has the cleansing word, or a person unconscious of the Father's using him for this purpose may speak the word that we need. We are to use these thoughts to unify our conscious mind with the superconscious; and at the same time these thoughts will wipe out error thoughts from the subconscious. Until we recognize and start this word of redemption, the Christ cannot come into our life with His good and abide, any more than the man Jesus could do mighty works in His own country while the people's hearts were closed against Him. We must make ready to receive the good that is in store for us.

Christ is always ready to give. Does He not tell us, "Behold, I stand at the door and knock; if any man hear my voice and open the door, I will come in to him, and will sup with him, and he with me." What a wonderful promise! What an opportunity to receive the highest that can come into one's life! Yet very few people still their mind enough to hear His knock, very few hold open the door long enough for Him to enter; they only let their thoughts bang back and forth like a loose shutter in the wind. They scatter their forces to the four ends of their universe, as the wind scatters the dead leaves of the trees in a storm. They concentrate on a thought or pray to God for a few minutes, and then they spend hours each day in thinking and living the exact opposite of that for which they have prayed. Here comes a doubt thought and it is considered; here comes a fear thought and it is considered. We speak words contrary to our prayer; and our action in disbelieving that the answer is already ours speaks louder than our words. Thus the thing for which we prayed is turned back to the Giver to wait until we are open to receive it.

The part of prayer called concentration is a

process of stilling the unruly or irrelevant thoughts so that our mind may give all its attention to the one thing desired. Until this is attained our prayers are like scattered forces that have little visible result. There is a commandment that reads, "Thou shalt have no other gods before me." Yet when we start to seek the silence to commune with God, we are like the Israelites bowing down to strange gods; we let all kinds of thoughts run riot in our mind to the exclusion of our holy thoughts. We start Godward in our mind, and immediately there come thoughts of Johnny or Susie, or of a neighbor, a customer, or a social event. We drift with these thoughts for a time; then call again to mind our holy thoughts, and in a moment, in our mind, we are starting down to the office, or on a shopping excursion, or planning the day's meals, or making over a dress, or perhaps outwitting a customer or a shopkeeper in some deal that is being considered.

Again we shake ourself and start Godward, but some duty of the day claims our attention. Finally we get up and go about our work without ever approaching the great white throne. We have wasted untold mental energy and unrecallable time, which if used in concentrated prayer would have given us peace and power and strength sufficient for the mastery of any task of the day.

When we are really interested in anything we give it our whole attention. You and I have many times become so interested in something we were doing that we did not hear the telephone, or the doorbell, or the call to dinner. This is the kind of interest we need when we start Godward in prayer. We would not call a book interesting over which we nodded and dozed, yet sometimes when we start to enter the silence and begin our prayer to God, we do doze, even fall asleep. In order to reach the Father, to speak to Him, to hear His voice we must be as vitally interested in our activity as was Jacob when he held onto the angel-presence until the break of day. He forgot all else, "I will not let thee go, except thou bless me," he said, and it was through this holding on until blessed that the great transformation from "supplanter" to "prince with God" came about.

During some such communion, forgetting self and everything except receiving a blessing from the Lord, we also shall get error conditions changed and attain perfect expression of that to which we cling, God, the good omnipotent. Pentecost came to the disciples when they were all together in one place, engaged steadfastly in prayer. The Holy Spirit will descend on us with great blessings when we draw together all our forces and worship God with our whole being, with all our heart, soul, and mind.

We do not concentrate on or hold fast to our holy thoughts in order to change God, for He is the same yesterday, today, and tomorrow, always waiting to give us that which He has prepared for us from the beginning. It is ourself that we seek to change by the holding of holy thoughts. We seek to cleanse ourself of doubts and fears, to build up faith so that we may be made receptive. We seek to make a clear path to Him over which our good may come back to us. Every holy thought held fast is the forerunner of some good yet to be ours, which is ours now if we are open enough to receive it.

The One who dwelt in consciousness continually with the Father and whose prayers were answered even as uttered said, "When thou prayest, enter into thine inner chamber, and having shut thy door, pray to thy Father." The

only way to close the door on unruly thoughts is
to hold a thought so holy, to become so interested in it, that the irrelevant thoughts will find
nothing in common with it, nothing to hold
them. They they will either go out and close the
door behind them or they will become so interested that they will be still and listen. If we resist
them and scold them they will push open the
door as fast as we close it. If we fight them they
will fight back, and the time will pass without
our reaching the holy of holies, without our coming into a consciousness of the glory of God and
having it clothe us with its richness.

When you are seeking the silence, take always
with you a very high thought so that you may
become quickly unified with the Father. Let it
drop from the head, the seat of the intellect, to
the region of the heart, out of which are all the
issues of life. If at first you do not get a realization of this experience repeat the thought: *Out
from this throne of God (heart) into all the
garden (body) flows the river of life (blood)
through all of its tributaries (arteries, capillaries,
veins), cleansing, healing, renewing as it flows.
Back to the throne flows the stream of life,
gathering up throughout the garden all the im-*

*purities, and whatsoever is unclean on its banks
is healed. It passes in review before the great
alchemist (the lungs), where the breath of God
applies to it a cleansing, vitalizing touch,
through which you become a living soul, born
anew in the physical, as you take with you words
and return to Jehovah.*

When the thought is thus dropped to the
heart, the whole being receives it, and you
become a mighty magnet to receive the good;
but when the thought is kept in the head, the intellect argues and reasons over it until it loses its
true meaning. Many a splitting headache has
come from the intellect's holding back the truth
of a thought from the physical universe, until
this thought has begun to hammer at the door
and demand its release so that it might become
vital in the living.

There will come a time, after we have truly
learned to concentrate on holy thoughts without
the intellect's interference, when the great subconsciousness shall have been cleansed. Then
praying will find its true place in the upper
chamber of the body, the top of the head. We
do not need to try to take our thoughts there, for
when we are ready for the day of Pentecost and

its baptism of power, the Spirit will descend on
us and we shall be lifted with it to this high
place. Until that time comes for us we are to
seek, to look steadfastly into God's heaven, so
that our thoughts may be of the purest form, our
words constructive and life-giving, and the acts
of our life productive of good only. Thus we shall
be confirming by signs this ministry to the race
consciousness, and we shall know and feel the
outpouring of the Holy Spirit upon us.

When we take a thought for the purpose of
concentrating upon it, we repeat it over and over
until it is fixed in our mind. We give it our un-
divided attention, becoming vitally interested in
it. We seek to have it become a very part of our
being; and indelibly written in our consciousness, it becomes one with us. Then it will
become powerful and draw to it others of its
kind. It will sink deep in the subconsciousness
and with its redeeming power reach all of the
dark corners of the soul, illumining them with
that true light which belongs to every person.

If it seems hard to hold to the thought until it
becomes a magnet within, it is well to practice
the holding of a thought—purely a mental process—for a minute, then two minutes, then five

or ten minutes, holding it to the exclusion of every other thought. When you can thus clarify your mind and hold your attention upon one thought, you are attaining the ability to concentrate that will lead to productive meditation. Only practice, patience, and earnest desire will give one the true power of concentration, which is interest and attention to the one thing that one desires to do or be. The accomplishment of this is the sure reward of all who repeatedly ask, earnestly seek, and patiently knock.

Let the light of Thy countenance, O Thou omnipresent One, continually be upon me, that I may be steadfast in my purpose of finding Thee. Let every thought of my mind become subservient to Thy thoughts, that my whole consciousness may be lifted out of darkness into that glory which I had with Thee before the world was.

Chapter V

MEDITATION

THE LAW OF God is written in man's heart more surely than it was written by the finger of God on the tables of stone for Moses, ''I will put my law in their inward parts, and in their heart will I write it.'' In the Psalms we find this definition of the law, ''Thy law is truth.'' The I AM or Christ within each of us is the Truth, and if we but turn within to this law of our being and make complete union with it, there is nothing more needed, for we shall find in it the fulfillment of all our needs, the consummation of all our desires, the righting of all our wrongs. This is what the Master sought to reveal when He gave the two great commandments as love of God and love of others, signifying the Christ characteristics that potentially belong to and exist in every one of us. It is this I AM or Christ within us that can say, "I have overcome the world."

Each of us, as we become conscious of the indwelling Christ and are governed in all our thoughts, words, and acts by the standards of the Christ, can declare and prove, "All authority hath been given unto me in heaven [mind] and earth [body]." It is through meditation on this rulership at the throne within that the promise is fulfilled, "I will . . . show thee great and difficult things, which thou knowest not." Great and greater will be the revelations of the omniscient Christ as we open ourself completely to Him and let Him have His perfect way with us. Greater and greater will be our understanding and use of the law hidden deep within our own soul as we sink the mortal thoughts in meditations on the Most High. The place of glory prepared for us from the beginning is only entered through prayer. Heaven is within, a place that we enter through thought.

Jehovah made many covenants with His chosen people. All who choose to serve Jehovah are His chosen people and are served of Him. This is the relation of reciprocity that the Master sought to reveal to His disciples when He took a towel and washed their feet. A covenant is an agreement or a promise of a blessing to be fulfilled by one party when the other fulfills his part. The covenant made by Jehovah with Joshua was that if he would meditate on the law day and night with the purpose of living according to it, Jehovah God would be with him wheresoever he went. Further, "then shalt thou make thy way prosperous and then shalt thou have good success."

The promise in the 1st Psalm to those who delight in the law of Jehovah and meditate on it day and night is that whatsoever they do shall prosper; they are likened to a well-watered, well-nourished tree that fruits every season. The Psalmist says that he has more understanding than all his teachers—"for thy testimonies are my meditation"—which was probably the difference between the intellectual understanding of the teachers and the spiritual understanding of the singer. David, beloved of God, whose inner meditations have sung themselves down the ages so that all who will may receive from them, says, "The law of Jehovah is perfect, restoring the soul" and he adds, "More to be desired are they than gold, yea, than much fine gold." He

ends this wonderful song of the 19th Psalm with
a prayer that each of us should voice often:

> *Let the words of my mouth and the*
> > *meditation of my heart*
> *Be acceptable in thy sight,*
> *O Jehovah, my rock, and my*
> > *redeemer.*

To meditate on a subject is to give it attentive,
earnest thought with the idea of having all its
meaning revealed; that is, all the meaning that
one is capable of receiving at the time. Aeons of
time are needed to reveal to us the deep mysteries of the kingdom, the fullness of which we shall
find only when we awake in His likeness, but
each moment we give to meditation on the higher truths reveals to us fresh glories. At any moment, in the night watches or in the midst of the
duties of the day, in any place, on a busy street
corner, at home or in the office, alone in the
open field or deep in the woods, one can drop all
outer things, relax from crowded thoughts and
activities, and sink down, if for only a moment,
into a holy meditation that will bring peace and
strength, refreshment in mind and body.

Isaac went out into the field at eventide to
meditate and, although we do not know what his

meditations were, we are told that in lifting his eyes he beheld his beloved. Suppose you seek to meditate in the open, and resting relaxed in the shade of a tree, you begin to meditate on the I AM or real self of you. As you meditate, the potentialities and powers of the I AM begin to open to you, and in this revelation all else is forgotten, the floating clouds, the rustling leaves, the song of birds, the hum of bees, even the creeping things. In your contemplation of your real self and its possibilities when realized, you lose contact with all things on the outer plane, things in which you are usually much interested. In meditation you are lifted up to behold your Christ self, the soul's beloved.

"I AM, I AM, I AM," the conscious mind repeats over and over, until the words become alive in your consciousness and take on their real power. They sink deep into your subconsciousness, erasing all personality as separateness. Both lifted up, the consciousness and subconsciousness become open and receptive to the superconscious mind, and from this high place is poured the glory of the I AM. The strength and power of the I AM! The love and tolerance and patience of the I AM! The justice of the I AM, the real me!

The wholeness and purity, the youth and beauty of the I AM, the Christ self! The wealth and wisdom, the courage and freedom of the I AM, the limitless I! The I AM, true self of me, God-created, made in God's image, after His likeness, given power and dominion over disease and death, over the environment, over the elements! I AM, Son of God, created to be fruitful and replenish the good, created to subdue all error! I AM, omnipresent, omnipotent, omniscient Christ of God. Let me behold Thee as myself!

At this moment, being lifted into the superconscious realm, we behold the beloved. To us comes the revelation that came to Peter (faith) when he faced the question, "Who say ye that I am?" and from within came the answer, "Thou art the Christ, the Son of the living God." Then do we know beyond a doubt that this revelation of the I AM has not come from the intellect, that flesh and blood has not revealed this to us but the Father within. We become thrilled yet strong and steady with the power of the I AM that possesses us. We become conscious that our I AM has made union with the great "I AM THAT I AM" and that our whole being is lifted to a higher plane. We have discovered a new heaven and a new earth and ever after shall our thought, word, and act be expressed from a higher consciousness of our real being. This is true meditation, and when constantly practiced will transform us into Christ's image from glory to glory until we awake in His likeness. This is the part of prayer in which we become ready for the way that leads us into the presence of God, to wait for His message to be revealed to us.

When we take a thought and meditate on it to the exclusion of all else, this thought becomes a power within us, a power for good or a power for evil, a power to upbuild or a power to destroy, according to the kind of thought it is. Many times a day we meditate on the things that are interesting to us; it does not seem hard; it seems the natural thing to do. It has been said that the mystics of India become so enrapt in their meditations that the birds build nests in their hair; poisonous reptiles crawl over them and do them no harm. Why? Because the mystics have dropped the personal ego, which has in itself fear, hatred, cruelty, prejudice. They have entered into the ego that is one with all life, one with divine love, and they are conscious of nothing else. When every cell in the body is taught to join the mind in its worship of the Highest, the time will soon come when nothing outside of us can distract us or disturb our communion with our God. The whole being—mind, soul, body—will then receive that which is needed to make us perfect, complete, powerful.

Concentration and meditation, when rightly practiced, do for our mental self what mastication and digestion do for the physical self: they give nourishment and growth. Concentration may be likened to chewing the food, preparing it; meditation to digesting it, using it. Concentration, like mastication, comes under our conscious control and, if rightly done, leads to powerful meditation, even as thorough mastication of food prepares the way for good digestion. A wise choice of thought is as necessary as a wise choice of food; then comes the wise use of it.

In true meditation one becomes joined with the Giver, contact is made with the Source of all good, and such faith, harmony, and peace are established in mind that through it the body and affairs are opened to receive. One holy thought meditated upon becomes a mighty magnet and draws to it other holy thoughts, which in their unity become so powerful that all opposition,

danger, sickness, poverty, and inharmony are
swept before them. The promise is that one shall
chase a thousand and two shall put ten thousand
to flight. Only in spiritual thought is this possible. Suppose that, so believing, you have a pre-
monition of evil, or think you are in danger, or
you fear persons or things; you will then immediately turn to Omnipotence and meditate on
the power of the One mighty to save, on His love
and His promise to rush to the rescue of all who
call on Him, believing. As you meditate you become lost to fear and enter into unity with His
love, power, and strength. You will feel His
presence enfolding you, and while you are in this
realization, any hand that may be lifted against
you will drop helpless and any danger pointing
toward you will be turned aside. To hold fast to
the angel-presence is to be led out of dangers, to
be held out of the way of all evil, no matter what
the seeming circumstance, condition, or appearance may be.

Premonitions and warnings come that we may
learn to hide ourself in Omnipresence, where
nothing of error-nature can penetrate. Thought
is the channel through which all fear enters; concentration upon or holding the fear thought

leads to meditation on it, and all kinds of fear thoughts flock in to possess us. This gives the thought power and strength to project itself in our world. It is the inner picture or film that takes on big proportions in our world if we let it become definite enough in the mind to become active in the life. Sometimes a tiny thought of fear is given so much attention—in concentration and meditation—that it becomes an obsession, a difficult experience to deal with for the one who has encountered it, which may entail much mental and bodily suffering unless he knows how to take the Christ in vision, thought, and word as the Leader and hold to Him only.

By changing the thought of fear instantly before entering upon concentration and meditation, and by giving high attention to the inner lordship, the I AM, we become identified with the power that is quick to dissolve error, and as we rest in this consciousness, fear with its power is taken from us. Nothing can enter our world except it find access through a thought of something similar that is already present in our mental world. Nothing can stay in our world unless it remains somewhere in our thoughts, and thoughts are meditations, even prayers.

Many times we really pray for a thing we do not desire by holding it in our mind in fear, holding it fast in worry, all the time begging and beseeching God to take it away, while we ourself will not let it go. We need to watch the fear and worry meditations and, when going to our Father for a need, put them far away, taking for meditation a thought that will leave the appearance far behind and make us feel, see, and know only God.

In deep meditation on a holy thought, the intellect retires, reasoning ceases, the emotions are stilled, the body forgotten. Even the thought with which the meditation started becomes absorbed in the other holy thoughts that it has attracted, as they flow in to possess us. It is but a step from this high attention to the one Presence and Power in the universe to the silence, the home of the soul; only a step into a four-dimensional or spiritual world where there is neither time nor space, personality nor place, where one waits for naught but for God to make Himself known.

Let the flaming sword of Thy presence, O God, ever guard the door of my mind, that only holy thoughts may take up their abode in me.

*Let Thy pure creations continually fill me—
mind, soul, and body—until I am lifted into an
abiding consciousness of my Christ self.*

Chapter VI

THE SILENCE

IN OUR TEXTBOOK, the Bible, it is recorded
of the time of Samuel, "The word of Jehovah
was precious in those days; there was no frequent
vision." Yet in one place the "lamp of God was
not yet gone out." In the temple (secret place)
the child Samuel ("heard of God") ministered
(waited) before Jehovah. There in the silence of
the holy place the boy learned, even as each of us
must learn, the attitude of mind that says,
"Speak, Jehovah, for thy servant heareth." He
learned, even as each of us must learn, to still the
self and wait and listen expectantly for God to
speak. As Samuel received a message direct from
Jehovah when he had learned to listen to God, so
shall we receive when we have made ourself

ready. We need to prepare.

Before this meeting with God in the night watches, Samuel knew only how to turn to Eli (Eli: "foster son" or intellect) for guidance and instruction. Two calls came from his God before he understood, but once he had recognized and heard the voice of God, nothing else satisfied him. The intellect in its proper place took instruction and was guided by intuition, the inner voice, for after asking and listening to the message that was given to Samuel in the night watches, Eli (intellect) said, "It is Jehovah: let him do what seemeth him good." Because he continued to seek from the only true source and was guided in all things by the One who spoke to him from the holy place, "Samuel grew, and Jehovah was with him." Through Samuel, Jehovah again appeared in Shiloh and made His teaching known so powerfully that none of His words was allowed to "fall to the ground." Samuel became the foremost figure of his age, a great prophet, serving God and being used by Him, always in close enough touch to hear and to be, as his name implies, "heard of God."

Many times it seems to us that we are living in an age similar to that of the boy Samuel and that the spoken or revealed word of Jehovah is precious (rare) because there is no frequent vision (looking Godward). The experience of Samuel is the experience of every soul, when on its way back to the Father's house it hears His voice, perhaps first unrecognized; then waiting expectantly, listening, we say as did Samuel, "Speak; for thy servant heareth."

There is no mystery about God speaking to man, there should be no infrequency of it; for man was created to walk and talk with God in sweet communion, in the garden of his soul. To anyone high or low, rich or poor, great or small who turns expectantly to the Father, asking earnestly and looking to Him only, there will come an answer if he is still enough. At any moment when there is a need, at high noon or midnight, in the crowd of a busy thoroughfare, or when alone far from civilization, in a consciousness of "Thou, Lord only" we can turn to the kingdom within for the answer. Shut away from conflict, from doubt and fear, we can there "rest in Jehovah, and wait patiently for him." From this inmost and high God will come the answer to any question, the supply for any need. We need only practice stillness, with our mind turned Godward, to experience such a calm, such a peace, such a joy that we recognize it is God's presence and wait eagerly for Him to speak. When the ear is opened Godward it shall hear, for the promise is, "Ask, and it shall be given you; seek, and you shall find; knock, and it shall be opened unto you."

The silence is not inertia, not a drifting into something we know not about. It is true, our body is relaxed, but it is alive and ready to act; our intellect is stilled, but it is alert and ready to be used. Through concentration and meditation on holy thoughts the mind is cleansed, and in a degree at least there is established within us the same mind that was in Christ Jesus, the mind that does know and can say, "I and the Father are one." Then we are ready to say meaningly, understandingly, and expectantly, "Speak, Jehovah; for thy servant heareth." These words are not to be directed to a presence without, apart, somewhere unknown, but to a living, vital, understandable presence within, as much a part of us as the germ of life is a part of the seed.

We need to remember the Master's last prayer to His Father-God for His followers, "that they may be one, even as we *are* one; I in them, and thou in me, that they may be perfected into one.'' We need to get a deeper realization of the indwelling Christ, for it is here within that we make union with the Giver; it is here within that we meet the Great Physician; it is here within that healing comes to us. It is here within that we sense a knower; it is here within that a voice gives us guidance, omniscient wisdom to use. When we recognize that whatever we need is within ourself, with the Christ, and when we turn here for our need to be fulfilled, the outer will take form according to the perfect pattern that the Christ holds. This perfection has been potentially ours always, but it is made plain to us at a time when we are silently waiting before the Creator. When we become open and receptive, it becomes in reality ours to have and to hold always.

When we come to the point in consciousness when we can say within ourself, ''speak Jehovah,'' we shall expectantly await the answer as a little child waits for the food for which he has asked and which he knows the parent will give him. The Master tells us that our Father is much more willing to give than is an earthly parent, but even God cannot give to those who come to Him with a consciousness closed by doubt and fear—closed through begging and pleading for the things that He is ever offering with outstretched hand—any more than a mother can give her child the bread and jam for which he has asked, if the child begs with his hands closed tight and held behind him. We should think this queer in a child, yet many grown people go to God, asking in the same way. This is the method of a chattering mind which thinks idle thoughts and speaks meaningless words during prayer.

A person in the silence must consciously cut out all noises, even the rattle of his thoughts and the murmur of his words, no matter how pleasing these sounding brasses and clanging cymbals may be to his intellect, if he would receive the great message the omniscient mind of God has for him. "Put off thy shoes from off thy feet, for the place whereon thou standest is holy ground" is as surely meant for us when we are seeking to enter the silence as was the great message that Moses received when God appeared to him.

All thoughts of the material we must leave behind—no matter how great our needs and desires—when we seek to enter the silence, for the material thought cannot find entrance to the spiritual realm. When we seek to enter the God presence filled with material desires, these desires close the channel through which the Giver ''presses out'' His gifts. ''Thou, Lord, only'' are the passwords that insure entrance to the storehouse of God, and we must use them in order to pass through the door into His presence. Ever the voice speaks to man, through turmoil in his activities, his trials and temptations, his joys and happy times. ''Be still, and know that I am God.'' Being still and knowing is sufficient for anyone in any time of need, for to know God is to know of His omnipresence, omnipotence, omniscience, and that for the sake of expressing Him we are even as He is.

As we enter the silence we are in the thought world. When we let our mind dwell on our desires, we attract thoughts that are relevant in character. These thoughts come from many minds, in many stages of growth, and sometimes we have unpleasant psychic (mental) experiences on the way to the silence. The radio fills the air with spoken words of all kinds. We can tune in as we choose, on the happy and foolish program, or on the lecture, the sermon, the concert. One thing that few of us realize is that within each of us is an invisible faculty, which may at any moment, unless controlled, tune in on thoughts. Our desires may attract to us the thoughts of others who have had like desires and who may have used evil means in trying to bring them to pass, and these thoughts, if we are drifting with our desires, may enter our mind and fill us with terror. We may suffer such an emotion of fear in this mental contact that it will be felt in our body and affairs. For this reason we should always take such a high and holy thought that it may have the power to carry us quickly through the mental realm to the great white throne. When we hold such a thought, nothing can touch our mental realm but thoughts of a similar kind, and with this thought as a light, guide, protector, the universal consciousness that surrounds us is cleansed for our passage.

Sometimes on this journey within us the inner ear is opened so that we hear voices. In our purity of thought we may touch a key that strikes the keynote of some sweet song of David or wise saying of Solomon. We may even pick up the words of the Lord Christ spoken when He dwelt among men. These come to the soul, to us, because of some need of strength or courage for the journey within or for our life in the outer. Perhaps we may hear the sweet tone of His loving voice saying, "Come unto me, all ye that labor and are heavy laden, and I will give you rest." Or it may be a reminder to us of the promise, "If ye abide in me, and my words abide in you, ask whatsoever ye will, and it shall be done unto you." Blessed are we when we become well enough attuned to Spirit to hear the teachings of the Christ, for then shall we begin to become like Him.

On this journey within, the inner vision may be so lifted that we may see with closed eyes such beauty of lights and colors as the open eyes have never glimpsed even in all the pictures that the invisible hand has painted to remind man of the glory of his spiritual home. The perfect rainbow, the glorious sunset, the forest afire with autumn colors are all pale as compared with the purity of the colors of the spiritual realm. Or again the vision may be of geometrical figures and shapes, all symbols of the harmony and order of the unseen world.

The physical may be spiritually roused during some period of relaxation and stillness until every part of it glows with the warmth of spiri-

tual contact and there extends out from the
redeemed body a beauty of holiness, an aura of
the brilliance of sunset colors, making one appear truly as a son of God; or vibrations may
shake every sleepy and darkened cell of inactivity
or disease into an expression of life, and never
again can the body function on a low plane.

Any of these or other pleasing experiences may
or may not be yours at some time when you are
standing on the threshold of the silence. They
are only symbols and signs that the senses are being lifted up into the spiritual realm, assuring
you of progress toward the attainment of spiritual consciousness. They are not to be sought
however, for our desire must be for the Highest—even to enter the presence of God. If any of
these signs do come, we should not seek to linger
on the threshold where we stand; but giving
thanks for this manifestation of spiritual growth,
we must seek to pass on into the greater beauty
and harmony that lies beyond, that we may no
longer see as ''in a mirror, darkly; but . . . face
to face,'' ''for we shall see him even as he is.''

When Elijah, fleeing in fear and jealousy, hid
himself in a cave (downward visioning), he was
commanded by the higher self to go forth and

stand on the mount (even rise above fear and jealousy for the work of the Lord). As he obeyed, seeking to follow the Lord into His presence, a strong wind rent the mountain; after the wind came an earthquake, and after the earthquake came a fire. But he found not Jehovah in any of these. After the phenomena had passed, there came the "still small voice," which Elijah recognized as Jehovah speaking. This recognition caused Elijah to wrap his face in his mantle (withdraw from the world of sense phenomena) and stand in the entrance of the cave (open his consciousness more positively toward God). Then and then only was he free enough of desires and emotions to receive the message from his God. It is only when we too are lost to emotion and desire, to thinking thoughts and seeing things, that we become "one-pointed" enough to hear the inner voice and receive its message.

You have at some time greatly listened. Perhaps you were alone in the deep woods and the crack of a bough startled you, causing you to stop; and forgetting all else—what you were seeking or where you were going—you listened intent on finding out if there was an unknown presence near you. Perhaps you were one of a

great audience, sitting spellbound under the
words of some fluent speaker, utterly unaware of
those who were sitting beside you, in your desire
to catch every word. Or you were so entranced
with the flutelike notes of some wonderful singer
that you found yourself on the very edge of your
seat in the intensity of your listening. Perhaps it
was in the night watches when you listened with
your whole being for the call of a little child or a
dearly beloved who might need you. Even more
absorbed will be your attention, your listening,
your stillness, even your alertness, when you
have truly entered the silence and are waiting to
hear the message from the Creator of your being.

It is in such stillness, such waiting before the
Creator, that the tiny sapling gathers the
strength to become the mighty oak, for strength
is for all creation. It is here that the flowers find
their glorious colors and beautiful forms, for the
beauty that the Creator possesses is for all that is
His. It is here that trees blossom and blossoms
fruit and form and ripen, it is here that the green
of nature finds its clothing; for all things find
their being in God's silence. Here also is the key
to our beauty of soul, our image and likeness,
our power and dominion, our perfection. In the

attitude of waiting we are receptive, and God makes Himself known in the form in which we are most able to receive Him. The assurance will come to us, as never before, that we are truly sons, joint heirs with Jesus Christ to all that the Father has. When we have entered this secret place often enough and abide long enough truly to behold the beauty of the Lord, it will spring forth as a living message of harmony in our life, a manifestation of wholeness, joy, abundance, and it will so fill our universe with the glory of God that all who cross our path or walk by our side will glimpse the God whose expression we are. Through the stillness of our being God will express Himself in the manifest plane: in our body, His temple, in our life, His activity, we shall express our likeness to Him.

O God, my Creator, my Father, let me become so still in body and mind, so free of desire and emotion, that my soul may enter Thy presence unburdened. Silently I wait before Thee, Thou omnipresent One. To receive again from Thee the glory that was mine with Thee in the beginning before the world was.

Chapter VII

THE MESSAGE

NO ONE CAN tell another person what is to come to him from the silence, what message he will receive from the One who dwells in the holy of holies within his own soul. No one can tell another what he will bring back with him into his life from the Creator of his being. Each one of us goes to God with different needs, in different states of consciousness, taking different steps in search of Him. Some go in roundabout ways, some go direct, each one preparing the path over which the message is to come back to him. Some dare to touch only the hem of God's garment, others go boldly to the throne of grace and kneel at His feet. During His earthly ministry the Master told His followers, "According to your faith be it done unto you." We receive according to our capacity, and the degree of our faith determines our capacity.

The Father always fills to overflowing any vessel that one of His children holds out to Him. He is not limited, neither does He limit us, but we limit Him in fixing our capacity to receive. We need to make greater our vessels for containing His love, we need to hold them steadier for Him to fill, we need to see them full to overflowing, as He would have them be. The receiving capacity of our vessels is always in proportion to the faith we have in the Giver's ability and willingness to give, in proportion to the expectancy we have of receiving that which we ask, in harmony with the vision we have of the finished, perfected gift. He reveals Himself in His fullness to those who entirely empty themselves of personality and let Him in His own way reveal to them that which they should know and do to become like Him.

When the widow, whose two sons were about to be taken for debt, went to Elisha for help, he asked her what she had in the house. She said a little oil (her faith), and he told her to go and borrow vessels from her neighbors (increase her expectancy from her knowledge of God's goodness). "Borrow not a few," said the one who knew God. Then she was instructed to take her sons (desires) and go into her room (the secret place) and close the door (wipe out doubts and fears) and pour (give thanks) into her vessels the increase of Jehovah. When the vessels about her were full, which she had borrowed according to the faith and expectancy she had of their being filled, she asked for more vessels. But there was none, "and the oil stayed." As long as there was a vessel to receive it, the oil continued to flow, even as our good continues to flow to us according to the amount of faith and expectancy we have. The widow's answer was the Father's "good measure, pressed down, shaken together, running over." She had asked for enough to pay the debt, and there was more, according to the prophet's words, "Go, sell the oil, and pay thy debt, and live thou and thy sons of the rest."

Many times we receive only partial answers to our prayers, and we cry, "Why are my prayers not answered as I asked? I had faith." But we have not added to the faith the expectancy and vision required to complete the work. We always receive full measure, according to the measure that we ourself provide for the reception of our good. If we desire to have our prayer answered in His full and running-over measure, we must ask, seeing the work already accomplished, as the Master said, "And all things, whatsoever ye shall ask in prayer, believing, ye shall receive."

The higher the soul reaches in its aspiration to find God, the greater will be the message, the richer the gifts. When we learn to pray the self-less, desireless prayer, sinking our will in the will of the Highest, assurance of the answer will be given us not only on the inner plane, but on the outer also. There is a covenant that we can enter into with the Great Giver: "All things that are mine are thine, and thine are mine." This promise of reciprocity will open up to us all that He is and all that He has, and there will be added to us that which is worth much in the bringing forth of His kingdom.

It takes a great hunger and thirst after God, an intense desire to be like Him, a sinking of self and desire in the will of the Highest, to enable us to find entrance into the most holy place and become a high priest to go in and come out before Jehovah. Jesus Christ, our great high priest, in whose footsteps we seek to follow in

order to reach the inner sanctuary, says, "Blessed
are they that hunger and thirst after righteousness: for they shall be filled." This filling may
take place in many ways. It always comes after
some waiting in faith and expectancy in the
silence, some waiting for the Beloved of the soul
to make Himself known. It may come as an inner
glory that quickens the flesh and shines forth in a
radiance such as covered Moses when he came
down from the mount of holiness, a transfigura-
tion that instantly cleanses and heals all the ills
of the body. The filling may come from entering
into God-Mind, becoming one with Omniscience, where all questions are answered and all
ways made plain.

Perhaps your "cup runneth over" as you sit
and sup with Him in the silence of your soul,
and you are filled with such a realization of the
richness of your Father's kingdom that the way is
made open for substance to flow into your life,
and every desire and need of your life is filled
full, to spare and to share. Or you may kneel
before the just judge in your desire to forgive
and be forgiven, and you are so filled with divine
love that ever after there will be manifested
toward you and from you a dissolving, redeem-

ing love so great that no man's mind or hand can
be lifted against you, nor your mind or hand
lifted against any man. When you enter into the
peace that "passeth all understanding," the
One who brought forth beauty out of the waste
and void and light out of darkness will make for
you all crooked places straight, all dark places
light, and your earth will blossom as a rose.

That of which we have need has a correspon-
dent in God's world of good—holiness, substance, harmony, peace, love, wisdom being
really what we need—and when we seek it, it will
be given to us in a usable outer form. When we
earnestly, prayerfully, joyously make our search
for the kingdom of God, putting aside all else to
accomplish our purpose, we shall find the kingdom, and we shall find that it includes all the
needs of mind, body, and affairs. The promise
is, "Your heavenly Father knoweth that ye have
need of all these things," and the promise goes
still further, "Thy Father who seeth in secret
shall recompense thee."

Spiritual deafness will cease when we really
cross the threshold into the silence, for the inner
ear will become alert in seeking to catch the message of the still small voice. The outer ear also

may be opened during some time of listening within for this message, so that "the deaf hear." Many a message will come to us when we have become still enough to enter the silence. It may be some great message repeated that the Master spoke when among men, bearing some new meaning and usefulness for us personally. It may be some individual message to comfort, to lift, to strengthen, spoken to us when the veil is lifted and we have passed beyond, into the holy of holies. Nevermore will we doubt the possibility of meeting God and walking and talking with Him in the secret place when once we have gone beyond the silence and seen Him face to face, holding sweet communion with Him in the garden of our soul.

A great tree falls in a place far from human habitation. It makes no sound, for there is no physical ear near enough to receive its vibrations from the air. The ear is the receiver of vibrations from the air and reports them to the intellect. It is thus we perceive what is called sound. In the silence we are not dealing with the physical senses, but with spiritual senses. We are not listening for the intellect, but for the voice of God. The "still small voice" speaking to us is soundless, yet conveys its message with a clearness beyond any spoken word of the human voice. When once this message is received, it is written indelibly in the soul and is even more readable to the one receiving it than is the largest print of a book to the physical eye. The more often this message is rehearsed, recalled, the more sure is the good to be gotten from it.

When we have learned to draw near to the Father, who sees in secret and rewards openly, with a heart full of faith and expectancy, we shall find that when the way seems dark and the shadows seem to close on us, we have only to reach out and take up the candle of the Lord, and the way will be illumined. If we calmly turn the question of knowing over to the omniscient mind of God when we come to a crossroad in life and are puzzled and worried about the way to take, the angel of His presence will direct our path, and we shall travel the right road, with this presence ever leading us on into greater good. When we can submit all seeming injustice to the just judge, when we no longer pass judgment according to appearances, His strong right arm will become our defense, and any hand lifted against us will drop in helplessness. Every lonely, homesick feeling, every craving of the soul seeking its home, a home not made with hands, will be filled to satisfaction with His loving presence.

Though family and friends forsake us, the Christ never will, for His promise, "Lo, I am with you always," is for all who will turn to Him, and these shall always find Him near and in that nearness be satisfied. When pain racks the body and we draw near to the Great Physician until we feel His loving touch, we shall arise and go forth renewed in mind, soul, and body, strengthened and healed. There is an omnipresent Surgeon to whom we can submit, in the silent place, any imperfection of the body, and who will rectify it according to the perfect Christ body. When bills mount up and the purse seems empty, we have only to turn to the One whose bank is unlimited, whose substance is for our use, and there wait in faith, and His abundance will be "pressed out" to us. Whatever the human heart craves, whatever the body needs, will be given in the silence, for whenever a cry goes from the heart Godward, He immediately answers, "Here am I." All this and still more unconceived good will unfold for us when we come in and go out no more but abide in the consciousness of the God presence.

The inside of the cup will be cleansed and the outside will show forth this cleansing in the radiant beauty of the living God, whose likeness we have become. Wherever we go we shall rouse in others a desire for the beauty of holiness that we express.

When our inner ear is attuned to catch His message even in the midst of our everyday living and working, and our inner eye is trained to glimpse His perfection even in the midst of appearances of error and inharmony, then our whole world will be filled with His glory. When we sit at His feet long enough to learn of him, we shall carry away with us His holiness, and even our presence, like the garment of the Master and the shadow of Peter, will be harmony and healing. Signs and wonders shall we do by stretching forth our hands in the name of the indwelling Christ. It is in the secret place, after we have felt the presence of the Most High, that we shall first join in that song of thanksgiving, started when the morning stars sang together in praise of the Creator and His creation, and evermore, when disappointment, discouragement, and downward visioning tend to overwhelm us, we shall remember this song which continually sings deep within and, joining in the anthem, be healed.

O Thou glorious Presence ever with me, let me sit at Thy feet until all darkness, all dimness of vision, has passed and I see Thee as Thou art. Let me listen until all spiritual deafness passes, that I may hold sweet communion with the Christ, my soul. I await now the fulfillment of Thyself in me, that I may express the glory of the risen Christ in my life.

Chapter VIII

LIVING THE LIFE

WHENEVER ANYONE enters the deep silence he loses himself in the cosmic universe and becomes one with the cosmic Christ. At the time of this merging of self with the whole, he is in a consciousness from which he can see his place as a part of the whole and in which he can receive his individual message. The entire man, mind, soul, and body, is then lifted in an ecstasy that breaks forth in songs of praise and thanksgiving, even magnificats such as come forth from a Mary soul rejoicing in being chosen a handmaiden of the Lord.

Coming back from a deep silence, filled with its harmony, ear still in tune with the inner message, eye still seeing the high vision, and the whole being thrilled from union with the Highest, we might think it would be easy to live the Christ life. But unless we steady ourself after coming back to the material plane, declaring that we are poised and balanced in Spirit and that as children of God we cannot be moved from His Truth of being, and realize this, we are apt to be thrown off our feet at the first sight and sound of an error appearance. Praise and thanksgiving should continue, for they have the power to bring forth that which is praised, and that for which we are giving thanks attains greater power to express itself, but we should not let it run to emotion. Emotion scatters; we waste ourself in it. Poised even during deep feeling, we experience the very strength and steadiness of the feeling holding us. "In quietness and in confidence shall be your strength."

Sometimes when a wonderful message has been given to us in the silence, we are content for days just to repeat it over and over, and live in the wonder of the inner revelation. Perhaps all at once there comes a great and burning desire to live the message, to make it true on the outer as well as the inner plane. Then this great urge within will carry us forward in the doing. A holy thought coming into a purified mind made ready to receive it must come to fruition. This is the "immaculate conception," and it comes only to those who have prepared themselves to receive the Holy Spirit and bring forth the Christ child. When once conceived in mind, the Christ child grows within the soul in wisdom and stature and meets with the favor of God and man. The growth within us and the expression without is always in accordance with the high watch we keep and the life we live, which is meat and drink for the Christ child's growth.

If one would grow, one must live whatever message is given in the silence. Unless the message from the Father becomes a living, vital reality in the daily life, seeking the silence becomes a mere pastime, a pretense, and hinders growth instead of hastening it. It is as much our mission to live any message given to us as it was the mission of Jesus Christ to live the life and die the death that He did. There is no message too trivial to be carried out, for if nothing in the outer seems to result from it, there has been built into the consciousness a willingness and readiness to do as directed that will lead to higher things. Naaman, seeking to be healed of leprosy, was wroth because the prophet (spiritual guidance) gave him so simple a thing to do as to bathe in the Jordan. He turned away, refusing to carry out the command, but his servant asked him whether, if he had been given a great thing to do, he would not do it. Naaman listened, and when he obeyed the prophet's command, his flesh became as the flesh of a little child, spotless, pure. On the other hand, the prophet's servant, as a result of disobedience to the law of righteousness spoken by the prophet to him, became a leper. God does not force anyone to do His will. He gives to each of us free will, the right of choice, but His law is that according to how we use the gift of choice, so will the manifestation be.

Jonah found himself in serious trouble by acting in opposition to the inner guidance. He found he could not place distance between himself and that within him which always seeks to lead man aright. He finally had not only to carry out the message but to extricate himself from that walled-in place, where his disobedience had placed him. The Psalmist afterward expressed that which Jonah found exceedingly true:

> *Whither shall I . . . flee from thy pres-*
> *ence?*
> *If I ascend up into heaven, thou art*
> *there:*
> *If I make my bed in Sheol, behold,*
> *thou art there.*
> *If I take the wings of the morning,*
> *And dwell in the uttermost parts of the*
> *sea;*
> *Even there shall thy hand lead me,*
> *And thy right hand shall hold me.*

This is the wonderful truth about the inner voice or intuition. It is always with us, no matter how far we may stray from our inner convictions, no matter how far from the path we may have wandered, no matter how high is the wall we have built between us and the way of righteousness. It is always waiting, ready and willing to guide us back into the way, to hold us steady as we find the path, to carry us forward in greater endeavor.

We each learn in some way, at some time, obedience to the higher self, that in us which is Godlike. It is obedience to this self, no matter how trivial the command, that prepares us to receive higher messages, that strengthens us for greater endeavor. It is the seeking to be a

workman approved of God, the handling aright
of the words of Truth, the living on the highest
level of the daily life that is worthy of being
trusted. Some of us cry out for work in the
Master's vineyard and we wonder why it is not
given to us when we are so willing to be used.
We do not give to a little child the responsibilities that belong to an adult. We feel that it
would hamper the development of the child,
even if he were capable of performing the work
as it should be done. Neither does the Lord of
the harvest give tasks to His workers that they are
not prepared to do, for the work's sake as well as
the worker's. There is no one who knows the
ability of any worker as does the One who is omnipresent, not even the worker himself. The field
is white for the harvest, and the workers are few.
The workers willing and fitted to do the needed
work of returning to its original perfection this
God-created, man-inharmonized universe are
indeed few compared with the seeming needs.
This realization alone should make each of us
eager to prepare ourself to take part in the work
of redeeming the race and its world.

The work of redemption, of carrying these
high thoughts and visions into the outer in words

and deeds that correspond, lies first within our own self. When we ourself are fit, then we are permitted to go to our neighbor: "Speak ye truth each one with his neighbor." This does not mean that in our enthusiasm for service we should seek to force the Truth on anyone. To be perfect every rose must be allowed to open in its own time, in its own way, and of its own accord. We can assist in attaining perfection by cultivating, watering, and fertilizing it, but never by forcing its petals apart. Each person must be given freedom to live his life as he would live it, not as another person would have him live it. Only in this way can he get the soul experience needed to bring him into full-rounded being in Christ, knowing the good because he has passed that way. There are no "flowery beds of ease" to carry us into the kingdom. Such beds are ours after we arrive, but on the way, there is great peace in having the Presence with us, great joy in the overcoming, and satisfaction from work well done, besides the happy companionship of those traveling the path with us.

If we would help another to arrive at our place on the path, perhaps assist him in passing us, our mission is to carry whatever message the Spirit

within us gives, to live the life according to the
high standard of life in Christ, to stand still and
be willing to wait, leaving the result to the
Father of us all. This takes courage; it takes patience, discrimination, love, unselfishness, tolerance, obedience, steadfastness, and above all it
takes faith in God as Father, healer, giver, lover,
guide and protector, judge and justice of our
beloved and ourself. This takes faith in each person in the world as being an anointed child of
God, whether he knows it or not, whether he is
expressing his divinity or not.

We need always to remember that no matter
what the higher self tells us to do, what the
message is that we receive in the silence, it is still
not too hard, even if the sense person does con-
sider it so. The power, strength, and wisdom
needed to carry the task through to perfect completion are always given with the message. It
only takes some initiative on our part to put
them to work. Here is the story not only of the
apostles of Jesus but also of the followers of the
omnipresent Christ—the command, the obedience, the results: "Go ye into all the world, and
preach the gospel. . . . And they went forth,
and preached everywhere, the Lord working with

them, and confirming the word by the signs that followed.''

If a person would have his prayers answered, he must be willing to be a channel through which the prayers of others are answered. If he would be healed, he must be willing to be a healer of discords. If he would have prosperity, he must be willing to give as freely as he desires to receive. He must not only be willing to do these things, but he must prove his willingness by doing them. If we look ourself squarely in the face, we shall find that many times the things we are asking for in prayer we are not trying to live in our life. We all know more of Truth than we live or try to live. To be open to receive, we need to express that which we are seeking to have expressed for us, we need to give as we would have the Father give to us, we need to forgive as we would be forgiven; in fact we need to practice the Golden Rule not only toward people but toward God also. Many a person has been healed at a time when he forgot his own aches and pains in praying for another's healing. Many a person has opened a channel for riches to flow to him by giving the widow's mite, which is not to be evaluated in terms of its size but in terms of what is in the giver's mind; as the Master said, ''She of her want did cast in all that she had, *even* all her living.'' Most of us give of our superfluity, of that which we do not need or want, or we give because of a mental necessity to give to God in order to be quite free in conscience. The tithe is the Lord's rightful share, but it is from that which we give beyond this law that we receive the greatest joy, if given in the Christ Spirit.

Sometimes a great urge, a message from the universal Mind, comes to us to give of our store to a certain work of the Father's or to one of His children. It may be one thing or another, perhaps a sum of money, the exact amount being named—for the Father knows the needs of His children and He is also capable of choosing the channel through which this blessing is to flow. We recognize the message and perhaps agree to it in our mind. Then we begin to cut it down until finally the Lord Himself would not recognize the assignment with which He had entrusted us. Perhaps we do not carry out any part of it after the intellect, with its reasoning and its citing of the contents of the pocketbook, is through with it. If we could only realize what we have done by our action! A great opportunity to be a channel through which the Father answers the prayer of another has been lost, a great opportunity to be a messenger from the Lord of hosts has been passed up. In not carrying out the assignment, we have closed ourself to some great good that was ready, waiting for us to prove our worthiness; for the Father never asks us to give for Him unless we are to receive back to us forty-, sixty-, a hundredfold, even an increase that is beyond our comprehending or receiving until we do give for the Master's sake. In many ways we find that God never withholds from us the good that we crave but that we ourself close the door through which our good is seeking entrance.

Whether we have consciously received a message in our silence, it has nevertheless been given to us. We never turn Godward, open to receive, but that the need in our mind draws forth from the Father a fulfillment of it in the highest form in which we are capable of receiving it. Our part is to step forth boldly in faith as if we were conscious of receiving. When the time comes for the question to be answered, for the conditions to be faced, for the need to be supplied, we shall find that it is met in overflowing measure by our Father's love. Words will be put in our mouth, wisdom will be given for decisions, strength to meet the occasion, and the needed amount of money will be forthcoming. It will all seem as natural as if the need had never existed; for even before we asked it was met, the fulfillment being subject only to our performing our part in the transaction. In the silence we contact the answer whether we are aware of it or not, and faith, expectancy, and steady vision bring it forth into being. Truly "faith apart from works is dead."

The condition of the body and the state of the affairs are living testimony, for all who will read, as to the kind of prayers we are offering; they are an outpicturing of our acceptance of the gifts of the great Giver. Health of the body, success, prosperity in the affairs, peace and harmony in the environment, freedom from accident, and joy in living are all outward manifestations in the life of those who practice the Presence, who pray without ceasing, who dwell in the secret place of the Most High. "The effectual fervent prayer of a righteous man availeth much."

Beloved, lift up your eyes until you behold the King in His glory, and truly you shall not have cause to say you are sick any more, limited any more, unhappy any more; for His beauty will become your beauty and the beauty of your whole world.

O Thou Christ of God within me, shine forth Thy light continually on my path, that I may not turn aside. Be Thou my guide every moment of every day, that I may follow in the footsteps of Thy Son. Give me courage! Give me strength! Give me faith! Give me love and patience and tolerance! I would follow all the way. I would cling to Thy glorified presence until I too become glorified and a shining light in Thy world. So let it be for me, Thy child, and for whosoever else may seek his inheritance of the All-Good.

The Meeting

And so I find it well to come
For deeper rest to this still room;
For here the habit of the soul
Feels less the outer world's control;
The strength of mutual purpose pleads
More earnestly our common needs;
And from the silence multiplied
By these still forms on either side,
The world that time and sense have known
Falls off and leaves us God alone.

—Whittier

Appendix A

MEDITATIONS FOR THE HIGH WATCH

THE SECRET OF health is in pure and harmonious thought. The secret of happiness is in the finding of the kingdom of heaven within. The secret of success and prosperity is in absolute trust in the Giver of gifts. The secret of the manifestation of all the good we need and desire, is in the high watch, the lifted vision. Our vision can only be lifted from the sordid, the low, from sickness and poverty and the many forms of error that seek to hold it down, by being filled with high and holy thoughts and by our holding fast to these until the eye becomes swift and single to the good only.

Error thoughts are continually seeking entrance into the mind. They are suggested by people and conditions about us. They spring out of the subconscious doubts and fears, hatreds and jealousies, poverty and failure, all of which we have stored away, some through the ages. They come from the race consciousness, the combined thoughts of all people. This is indeed a formidable array of error causes, and it can be handled by no man alone, for it is subject only to the Christ. Error and its results are continuous in the life of everyone until we come to that point in our development where we are willing to redeem and build anew. When this process starts, we seek through our conscious mind to cease forming opinions and conclusions based on appearances, and we turn to God-Mind for guidance in all things. In this way not only is the good of the present accomplished, but the subconsciousness is cleansed and refilled with high and holy thoughts—old error thoughts are wiped out and a new and higher future is established. Thus the whole being is lifted up into higher and holier living, and an impenetrable wall is built around us that protects us from outer errors.

Until a person becomes poised and balanced in Spirit he cannot always, under great stress and strain, lift the vision alone. He may be on the way but not yet so conscious of the indwelling Christ that he can turn to Him for every need. His ear may not yet be attuned to catch clearly the message from the superconscious Mind, for the intellect still reasons and friends suggest, all of which distracts his attention from listening within. His eye may not yet be pure enough to see the good only, for appearances seem distracting and real, and they create pictures in the mind from which thoughts form. Until the time comes when a person of himself can turn quickly to God, there are always answers provided by the omnipresent One to meet his asking, seeking, knocking. It is in the receiving, in answer to the asking, in the finding through seeking, in the opening to the knocking that the Father blesses us, whatever the method, whoever the channel.

The meditations in this little book have been given to the writer in various times of need, to be used for herself or for someone seeking help through her. They came not from herself but as the voice of the Christ speaking through her, to bless and to fill those who did "hunger and thirst after righteousness." These meditations are now given to you in order that they may be a blessing and a means of filling many hungry and

thirsty souls who are seeking the righteous way in
like times of need, as a means of lifting their vision from the material to the heavenly. Use them
for yourself in time of need. Use them for the
world, sending them out into the universal consciousness so that whosoever will may receive, so
that the whole human race may be lifted into a
higher consciousness and a better expression of
life.

To read a holy meditation over and over and
over again, perhaps to memorize it, is to be filled
with its holy thoughts both in the conscious and
the subconscious mind. The vision is lifted; we
enter the high watch. Fears and doubts vanish,
faith is increased, strength is gathered, power
prevails. That which before seemed such a formidable giant, now sinks into nothingness. It
has been dissolved by the change in consciousness that took place while the words were being
repeated. From this new state of consciousness
come healing, success and prosperity, joyful and
harmonious living.

The more often one enters the secret place to
meditate on holy thoughts, the more does one
become like the Christ. When a person has
entered often enough into the holy of holies and

remained long enough, his mind will become so filled with its purity and holiness that no longer will outer errors change it. Then there will be no more going out and coming in. He will have arrived! He will abide! Praise God!

Meditation of the High Watch

I keep my eyes ever single toward Thee, Thou King of Kings, Thou Lord of Lords, toward Thine omnipotence, omnipresence, omniscience, toward Thy love and strength, Thy beauty and purity. I let Thy joy fill me, Thy perfection heal me, Thy wisdom guide me, Thy substance feed me.

Because my eyes are toward Thee I see only my lordship, my kingship, my likeness to Thee, and this vision of my perfection takes form in my outer world. I express my likeness to Thee in my flesh, for I see in my body the perfection of a little child recently come forth from Thy bosom, pure, perfect in form and function, a Christ child. I see my strength as the strength of a great oak that has grown tall and broad and sturdy through always sinking its roots deeper in Thy substance, pushing its boughs out in Thine omnipresent life, whether the winds blow it, the rains beat upon it, the sun scorches it. I see in my life the glory of the flowers that draw their perfection of form and color from omniscience, keeping to their pattern within, whether they are surrounded by beauty or ugliness, whether their neighbors are distorted or perfect. I see my supply "pressed out" from Thy living substance, and as lavishly provided for me as the air I breathe, as the blades of grass that my feet touch, as the leaves that drift down on me from the autumn trees.

Through my divine inheritance from Thee I have power and dominion over sickness, poverty, all inharmony. As a fulfillment of my inheritance, I live as Thou would have me to live—unafraid, undaunted, victorious, trusting Thee utterly, expressing Thy perfection in all that I do and say. I see all Thine other children as I see myself, heirs to Thy glory, partakers of Thy good.

I give thanks to Thee, O Keeper of the High Watch, for Thine omnipresence, omnipotence, omniscience always with me as my own, giving me courage and strength and power to keep my eyes single toward Thee, and Thy holy will expressing itself through me, Thy child.

A Meditation for Relaxation

Father, as I come into Thy presence I lay aside all human likes and dislikes, all sense desires and flesh emotions. I cease struggling after things, cease striving. Knowing that I am Thy beloved child, I am free from worry and anxiety. I am not fearful of anything or anybody, for underneath and about me are Thine everlasting arms. I forgive as I would be forgiven, for my heart is filled with a realization of Thy redeeming love. A greater understanding of all life comes to me as I sink down in quietness with Thee. My soul rests in peace and is glad.

In this union with Thee the intellect loses its disposition to doubt and argue. My mind is ready to think Thy thoughts after Thee, and in this state of mental relaxation my body receives its release from the bondage of error thoughts. From the crown of my head to the soles of my feet, every cell and every nerve relaxes and lets go of its tenseness. My head—eyes and ears and mouth and nostrils—relaxes and lets God-life flow in freely and fully. My limbs relax, the bones and flesh relax, the muscles and nerves and skin relax, all open and subject to the renewal of their Creator. All the organs of my body relax so that they may do their work in divine order and harmony, performing their perfect functions in building the Christ body. The emotions are quieted and transformed into new life that is both soothing and thrilling. My heart is at peace with God and man and beats in unison with the great heart of the universe. The breath of God in my nostrils makes me a new creature in Christ Jesus, every whit whole. The river of life circulates freely through a renewed and released body, cleansing every cell, and renewing me according to the divine pattern.

As Thy spirit of peace and love pervades my whole being, all that was weary in me is refreshed, all that was sick is made whole, all that was limited is made free and full. I am recreated in mind, soul, and body. I am released from the bondage of graveclothes and come forth into the glorious Christ resurrection!

"Bless Jehovah, O my soul,
    And all that is within me, *bless* his holy name."

New Year's Eve Meditation

The book of the passing year is spread out before me as I sit alone tonight. Whatever wrong of another toward me that has been written on its pages I forgive and wipe out. Any wrong of mine, intentional or unintentional, I myself forgive, and I open myself to receive forgiveness from anyone whom I may have offended. I let all hurts, all self-pity, all selfishness, all fear, all hate, all sickness and poverty thoughts become as water that has passed away.

The book of my life is cleansed from cover to cover through the forgiving love of Jesus Christ. It is therefore without spot or blemish.

I ask, my Father, that before I enter into the new year the Spirit of the Christ may so fill my heart and soul that all the pages of the book throughout the year to come may be filled only with that which I delight to keep in the chamber of my memory and see fulfilled in my life. Let all the spiritual joys of the year that is passing be increased, let all the rich thoughts multiply, all the good sent from me and toward me grow. Let faith, beauty of soul, compassion, and love become in me as they were in the Nazarene. Let me grow in wisdom and stature and in favor with God and man.

At this closing of the old year I consecrate the incoming year to Thee, and myself to Thy service. Use me, Father, in Thy vineyard; use me, mind, soul, and body. Use all the material goods I possess for the setting up of Thy kingdom on earth through the upliftment of Thy children. Let me be a peacemaker, a healer of discords, of poverty and fear thoughts. Let me open the eyes of the blind to Thy beauty, the ears of the deaf to Thy message. Let me point the lame and the halt to the path wherein they can run and not be weary, walk and faint not.

Let me express only the Christ every moment of every day the whole year through, and let the Christ in me call forth the Christ of everyone who enters my life or crosses my path in the time to come.

My Banker

Father, Thou art my banker. Before I came into being Thou did deposit to my heavenly account with Thee an unlimited supply. Throughout the ages there has never been any lessening of Thy gift. Because I have not been conscious of this bountiful provision for me I have used sparingly of that which Thou would have me use in abundance. I have not realized that the inflow that Thy law establishes is equal to my faith in the providing law and my free use of its gifts.

O Thou great Giver, I know now that wherever and whenever there has been emptiness, lack in my life, it has been because I have held poverty thoughts, have seen lack, which has closed the way to the entrance of Thy stream of substance always flowing toward me. Now I know that Thou do not limit me, but that every thought, word, and act that do not correspond to Thy bountiful provision for me shut out Thy supply from my manifest world.

Father, let me become each day more conscious of Thy loving care for me, Thy beloved child. Let me realize more and more the greatness and permanency of Thy provision for me. Give me greater faith and wisdom and love, that I may use freely and wisely from Thy storehouse to satisfy every need and desire in my life and in the lives of others of Thy children. Let me become conscious that the more I use in Thy name, the greater becomes my capacity to receive.

I give thanks, O Giver of gifts, for an overflowing measure of substance ever ready to meet my demands, for the harmony and beauty and richness that accompany the conscious use of gifts direct from Thy hand.

Divine Love

Divine love in me is a consuming fire, utterly destroying from my mind all thoughts of hard conditions, all hard thoughts toward others, and destroying also all hard thoughts of others toward me. Love sweeps clean from my consciousness all hardness of every kind, past, present, and future, and eliminates from my body consciousness all hard manifestations. Warts, corns, calluses, lumps, gallstones, knots, hardened arteries are all cast out by the forgiving love of Jesus Christ accepted by me.

Divine love in me is a lubricating oil, dissolving all criticism, hate, selfishness, condemnation, worry, anxiety, envy, self-pity from my mind and their resultant conditions from my body. In the love of God I live, move, and have my being; rheumatism, neuritis, stiff joints, indigestion, valve weakness—all these disappear in the sweetness that love is, that I am.

Divine love in me is a radiant light that shines out before me, making plain my way, guiding me in the ways of wisdom, illuminating the path for others; a light that constantly lifts higher my consciousness, drawing up my body organs from all fallen conditions; a light that no darkness of any kind, no disease or accident can dim; a light that gives out to others and draws from others to me justice and righteous judgment.

Divine love in me is a mighty magnet that draws my good from the seen and the unseen. Joys seek me, friends flock to me, health and wealth make me their home, as the Christ Spirit within attracts to me that which is in its own likeness.

Divine love is the God spark within me through which I express compassion, tolerance, and patience toward all.

I am divine love, supreme, eternal!

Meditation on Substance

I am relaxed and still. Worry, anxiety, fear, and doubts drift off into the nothingness from which they come. Trust enters, peace prevails. I touch the hem of Thy garment, O Christ, and all poverty thoughts are healed. My eyes are opened and I see substance everywhere. It spreads out before me greater than the expanse of the ocean and of the dry land, greater than all the oceans and dry lands of the multitudinous planets, for it is not confined, not limited by three dimensions; it is of the Spirit world, unlimited, eternal. It surrounds me as the air I breathe and fills me as the life I feel. It is thought for my mind, food for my body, supply for my needs.

With infinite love the great Giver has created substance for His child, who I am. He has given me the power to mold from it all my desires, to fill all my needs, the power to be a channel through which it flows into His universe to make all waste places fertile. Day after day, year after year, age after age, I and millions of others of His children have used His substance in limited quantities, not realizing that it was ours to use in abundance. I see it now overflowing all creation.

The more I use it, the more it flows to me, and still it is as if it never had been touched, for its vastness is now comprehended only by the mind of its Creator.

I praise and give thanks for the garment of substance with which the Father clothes all His creations. I praise and give thanks that He clothes and provides for me, His highest creation, His dearest possession, measuring His good out to me with a measure that overflows all previous ideas of opulence, all former manifestations of abundance.

As I go back into the material world to the duties of the hour I take with me this realization of substance as my eternal birthright, my everlasting heritage, my omnipresent possession. I hold fast to this high vision until all my outer world manifests this inner opulent perfection.

My Work

I thank Thee, Father, for the work that Thou hast given me to do in Thy busy universe. I do not seek to shirk my task; whatsoever my hand finds to do I do to Thy glory, that it may be done and may accomplish the purpose for which Thou did give it to me.

When my work is to take a towel, as did the Master, and serve others, then Thou dost give me power to serve sweetly, serve well. When I need wisdom and understanding to carry on, the Knower within gives me sufficient to meet the need of each hour. When I labor with my hands, Thy strength is made perfect in my human weakness.

I know that as my work is finished on one plane I shall hear Thee say, "Well done, good and faithful servant; thou hast been faithful over a few things, I will set thee over many things; enter thou into the joy of thy lord." I know that when the Adam consciousness of earning by the sweat of the brow has passed from me, I shall enter into the Christ consciousness of speaking into manifestation all my needs and desires. I hasten this time by doing all that my hand finds to do as unto the Lord. I seek to make of myself a worker that need not be ashamed, approved unto God.

Let me while doing my work, whatever it may be, spare the time to be kind. Let me be a blessing to whoever works by my side. Let those who

cross my path go on with a lifted vision.
Let me glorify work.

Forgiveness

All things, past, present, and future, that are out of harmony with the divine law are forgiven me by the One who gave His life to set me free.

There is no transgression, no sin of omission, no sin of commission that Thou, O Son of man, O Son of God, hast not wiped out for me in Thy "Father, forgive them," spoken from the Cross.

Ignorance in transgression, willfulness of desire, and all their effects have become as nothing as I enter upon the "crossing out" with Thee, my Savior.

Scars and wounds and hurts are made whole; both those which I have received and those which I have inflicted have been healed by Thy blood shed vicariously for the healing of the nations.

All unforgiveness in me and toward me, all intolerance and injustice, even that present in the lives that I remember no more, are completely blotted out through Thy forgiving love, O Christ of God.

I accept Thine atonement, O Lamb of God, Messiah of the world. Through Thy redeeming love I am washed clean, rising above all human appearances, all material bondage.

Now am I resurrected from the dead in mind, body, and affairs, and enter into the newness that has become mine through Thee. I am a child of the living God, the Word of God made flesh.

Meditation for the Night Watches

I am alone with Thee in the darkness of the night, but I neither need nor desire any other presence. As I feel Thy nearness, all darkness, all dimness of vision depart and the glory of Thy countenance shines round about me. My soul is filled with Thy radiance, my mind is lifted above all fear and worry, my body is free from the bondage of pain. No more am I sad, no more am I lonely, no more am I anxious, for I have found perfect trust in the goodness of Thy will for me.

I give myself and my loved ones, my all, into Thy keeping, my Beloved. I know that the morrow will bring the solution to every problem, the answer to every question, the supply to every need. Until then I do not need them. I need only Thee. In Thine arms I find peace; under Thy wings I am secure. I lose myself in Thy Self, and in the sweetness of this oneness with Thee I rest and rest and rest until the coming of a new day.

The River of Life

There is forever flowing to us the river of life. It issues forth from the sanctuary of God, pure, crystal-clear, redeeming and vitalizing in its nature. It is a fountain whose waters never fail, it is a well of living water springing up unto eternal life. Its waters are for the healing of the nations through the cleansing and purifying of the individual. It is without money and without price for those who thirst for God, the living God. Those who drink of these waters shall never thirst again.

I enter boldly into the waters of this river of

life; in confidence I lie down in the stream. I surrender my wounds, my mental and physical pains, to its purifying and renewing action. Knowing that Thou art with me, I pass calmly through the waters. The rivers shall not overflow me, but when the cleansing is finished Thy hand shall draw me forth out of many waters.

I invite the peace of this river to enter in, that my soul may become as a watered garden. I invite its purity to enter my mind that it may be as a city of God made glad. I invite its tributaries to break out in all the desert places in my life that they may blossom as the rose, in all the waste places that they may become a Garden of Eden, in all the wilderness that it may be filled with beauty, in all the lonely places that they may resound with melody. Everything shall live whenever the river flows; everything on its banks shall be healed. My blind eyes shall be opened, my deaf ears shall listen and hear, my lame mentality shall leap into livingness, and the whole shall break forth into a song of "Glory to God in the highest."

I am a channel of the living fountain that comes forth from the throne of God. I give of my waters and am never depleted, never impoverished, because I am aware of my Source. I know that he that waters shall be watered also, and I give myself as a channel through which the living waters flow to all humanity.

Meditation for One Seeking a Position

There is no lack of a place for me to serve in this great busy universe that Jehovah God created. When it was created, I also was created, and the Lord of Creation created with me all my good, all that I should need from the time I started out on my journey from Him into experience until I returned to Him, knowing as He knows and seeing as He sees. Thou, O Father-Mother God, hast always provided for me bountifully all that I would receive. Even now Thou dost stretch out overflowing hands to me.

There is a place prepared for me. Before I go forth to find this place I enter into Thy consciousness of all good. I fill myself with Thy glory of expression and let it shine forth from me. I recognize that I myself am success, and that my good is seeking me. As I go forth to enter my place, I know that I am about my Father's business, and that the angel of His presence has already gone before and made plain and successful the way.

In seeking my own I let no words of others discourage me. I let no acts of others hurt me. I keep my vision steadfast on the Giver of gifts that I may see clearly the way that He points out to me. I keep my ears attuned to the "still small voice" that I may hear when He says, "This is the way, walk ye in it."

All past thoughts of not enough pay, too hard work, lack of knowledge are wiped out. All careless work, unproductive work, uninspired work is forgiven me. I know that I have that which I earn, and I use my spiritual knowledge of true service to increase my receiving capacity. I seek henceforth to give to my work more than I earn, and the overflow returns to me with its increase, even as the needle returns to the magnet.

Right now is the time predestined from the beginning for me to enter into higher work, because now I have lifted myself above losses, above lacks, have ceased to depend on positions, possessions, persons for my substance.

I praise and give thanks, Thou Giver of gifts, for the beauty with which Thou art filling my life, through this new service which Thou hast given me to do. I thank Thee, Father, for service, all-absorbing, uplifting service, where I can preach the gospel of good will, health, peace and plenty, by the life I live and the work I do.

Easter Meditation

Christ is risen in my soul today, and every cell and fiber of my being enters into this resurrection. I feel the thrill of new life as it pulses through and through me. I am released from bondage. I am alive in Christ Jesus.

O Thou Son of God, I thank Thee for becoming a son of man, for taking on bodily appearance that Thou might prove to the race that flesh has no power over Spirit. I thank Thee for Thy great love for all, *for me,* which carried Thee through Gethsemane, up Calvary, and into the tomb so that it might count as an atonement for all who follow Thee. Lead Thou me on, O Way-Shower. Let me ever submit my will to the will of the Highest; give me strength and courage to bear the burden up my every Calvary; let me continually cross out the little self until it is forever crucified; let me feel Thine all-sufficient presence with me as I enter the tomb of any experience. Let me know, Thou omnipresent Christ, that once for all Thou has passed through death so that all others may rise out of sin, sickness, poverty, ignorance, and death into the fullness of a new life of glory.

I am not afraid of Gethsemane; it is only letting go of the perverse human will so that the good of God's will for us may become manifest. I am not afraid of calvary, for it is only an opportunity to prove the willingness of the great Burden Bearer to carry our burdens. I am not afraid of the cross, for I know it is only the place in consciousness where I give up the lesser self so that the Christ self may rule my life. I am not afraid of the tomb, for I let it become to me as the secret place of the Most High, where I may hide whenever error approaches. There, alone with Thee, O risen One, I become so filled with Thy peace and power, so alive to the Church within, so conscious of my oneness with the Father that I can come forth into the world and say to all error, "Touch me not; I am risen."

The Savior of the world is not dead; He is risen. He walks with me, He talks with me, He directs my way, He provides for my every need. He leads me through the valleys to the very mountaintops. He shines through me so that men may see His risen glory and follow also after Him through the valleys and on His ascension to the heights.

Let the life in plant and tree break the bondage of silence, let the birds join in the melody of the Resurrection, and all the creatures be glad. Let people recognize the power of their likeness to Thee, and lift up mind, soul, and body in an ecstasy of joy as they join all creation in the glory song, ''Christ is risen! Earth is now redeemed!''

Purse Blessing

I open my purse and there is poured into it the substance of God. I turn it upside down and pour out some of its contents wherewith to bless that work of His which the Father points out to me. I use all that I need freely but wisely. Yet my purse is never empty. It is constantly being filled from that eternal substance of Spirit which is without beginning, without end. This substance overflows my purse, and the more I use from it the larger the stream flowing into it becomes. I thank Thee, Father, for substance ever taking form for the use of Thy children everywhere.

Morning Meditation

I awake to this day, a new day, a new opportunity, born again in the night sabbath of my soul. I arise with praises to Thee, O Creator of my being. As I remember my likeness to Thee, my mind and my body sing, "Wake up, my glory, awake!"

As the glorious sun rises above the horizon and floods my material world with its light, so the "sun of righteousness" rises in my consciousness to fill my soul with its glory, with a radiance that shines throughout my universe.

I thank Thee, Father, for the day spread out before me, with its opportunities for service to Thee. Thy wisdom shall lead me, Thy beauty fill me, Thy substance provide for me throughout this day and all days to come.

While the day is yet new I give myself to Thee, Father, with the single desire of being a channel through which more of Thy beauty, wisdom, joy, love, and substance may flow into the hearts and lives of Thy other children who cross my path or walk by my side today. Let me express so much of Thee in my conversation and acts that all who see and hear may recognize that Christ is my pattern and seek also to follow after Him.

Today let me see beauty everywhere. Let me see the Christ in my fellowmen. Let me call forth the Christ expression wherever I walk; let me call it forth in loving-kindness from person to person and from person to God. Let me call forth peace and harmony and joy. Let my whole world be filled with gladness, because I have today lived and walked with God.

Through Thy presence with me, all that I do this day succeeds, for whatever I undertake within Thy will is filled with Thy wisdom and substance and life.

For the Homekeeper

My home is a heaven for my loved ones, for I

guard it from every enemy of happiness that
seeks to enter. Above its portals I inscribe:
   None enter here but in love.
   None leave here except in peace.
      On its walls I write:
   Christ is omnipresent in this house-
      hold.
   All members of this family put their
      trust in Him.
I wipe out selfishness, inharmony, discontent,
worry, anxiety, fear from my heart and see each
member of the home free also from these errors,
through a realization of the Christ Spirit within.
I think and speak only in terms of plenty, for I
know that in substance there is always overflowing abundance, and I fill the pantry, I fill the
closets, I replenish the home with furnishings
from God's substance, created for our use from
the beginning.
   I dust out disease germs, contagion in
thought, as I dust my treasures. I stir in love and
substance as I prepare my food. I darn and mend
and sew, realizing that robes of righteousness
that never age are gifts to those who abide in the
house of the Lord.
   I am not cumbered about much serving but

take time to sit at the feet of the Master and learn from Him how to meet every situation with wisdom and love, how to heal the sick within and without my portals, how to receive strength for the day's duties, and how to keep sweet under all circumstances.

I send my family forth into the world surrounded by love that protects, strength that sustains, courage that succeeds. I welcome them home with a love that fills them with peace and contentment.

"I can do all things through Christ which strengtheneth me," serving with gladness, being served in turn with joy. Cooperation, kindness, and harmony reign supreme in this household, and my loved ones and I work together to establish the kingdom of God on earth.

Room Blessing

I hallow this room by establishing within it the living presence of the Christ. In His presence there is nothing to fear. Good only abides here, and my room is filled with an atmosphere of peace, joy, life, health, and opulence. They sing themselves into my body and out into all my affairs. When I leave this room the angel presence keeps watch over my treasures, yet it goes before me to guide and protect. When I return the presence enters before me with peace and love, yet it was always there. It is Omnipresence, the same yesterday, today, and forever, in which I live and move and have my being. My whole world is filled with its glory now and evermore.

The Supreme Remedy

Thou dost walk by my side, Son of God, Redeemer of the world. Thou art the supreme remedy for my every lack, the cure of my every longing. Thou art the ease for every heartache, the satisfaction of every desire. Thou art my healer, my banker, my guide, my all in all. There is no need in my life which Thou dost not completely fill with Thyself.

Through every moment of every day down the ages since I came out from Thee into expression, Thou hast kept me. Thou keepest me still in the hollow of Thy hand. Thy love overshadows me in all my wanderings and guides me back into the righteous way. It goes before me to make my way light; it remains behind me to protect me; below it lifts me up out of hard places. It plucks my feet out of the nets of materiality and sets them on the rock of salvation. Its bountiful table is always spread before me, until my cup runneth over.

Thine all-encompassing love has kept me back from many stumblings, has held me back out of many waters, has emancipated me from fear and doubt and worry, from sins of omission and commission. Thy love is from everlasting to everlasting, the same yesterday, today, and forever, and in it I live and move and have my being. In it I find completion, I find peace and satisfaction.

Because Thou art through eternity the supreme remedy for every lack in mind, body, and affairs, I hold to Thee only, and am transformed from glory to glory into the spiritual unity with Thee that was mine before the world was. Thou, O Christ of God, art the way, the Truth, and the life, and Thou hast Thy home in my soul. I give myself to Thee as an eternal gift, and in this union I lose all resemblance to the old Adam man, for I am a new creature in Christ Jesus, whole, complete.

Table Blessing

Thou unseen Guest, increase this manifestation of Thy living substance, as Thou did increase the loaves by Galilee, until every hungry
need of our mind, body, and affairs is filled to
overflowing. Amen!

Child's Prayer

Father-Mother God, I thank Thee for Thy
angel-presence keeping watch over me by night
and by day, helping me always to do right, pro-
tecting me from all harm. I thank Thee for the
Christ within that keeps my mind pure and
makes my body strong. I thank Thee for Thy
gifts of peace, health, and abundance poured
out to my loved ones now and evermore. In the
name of Jesus Christ, Amen!

Song of Praise and Thanksgiving

My heart is singing a song of praise and
thanksgiving to Thee, my Beloved. My soul

drops all sorrow and sadness, that the song's lilt may reach every cell of my body and my whole being be lifted up in a chorus of gladness to Thee, my Creator, my Keeper.

For the many blessings as yet unmanifest that Thou, O Giver of gifts, hast prepared for me when I am ready to receive them I give thanks. For the blessings of today, to which I have full and free access and which make my life happier and holier and more productive of good, I give thanks.

I praise and give thanks for Thine omniscience, for the wisdom and right judgment that fills my mind and works out in my life, as I seek to be guided by the will of the Highest.

I praise and give thanks for Thy rich substance and the bounty with which Thou dost fill my hands as I hold them out in faith and expectancy to Thee.

I praise and give thanks, Thou Great Physician, for the healing stream of life that is ever cleansing and healing my body as I submit it to Thee for renewal.

I praise and give thanks for the angel of Thy presence, omnipresent One, a pillar of fire when the way seems dark, a cloud of hiding when I need protection, ever omnipotent on my path back to Thee.

I praise and give thanks, O Lover of my soul, for Thy likeness of love, even the living Christ within me, shining from me toward others. I thank Thee for the words and deeds that are made possible through the tolerance and patience and justice of Thy love in me and in Thine other children.

I thank Thee for a home whose foundation is laid by the Master Builder, for loved ones in whom I know dwells the Christ of God, for work that is a joyful service to Thee. I thank Thee for blessings manifold, for the beauties of nature, for the fellowship of friends, for the opportunity to serve Thee.

I thank Thee that I am because Thou art and that I am what I am because Thou art what Thou art. I thank Thee for this consciousness of unity with Thee. My soul is glad, my heart rejoices, and all that is within me blesses Thy holy name.

A Christmas Eve Meditation

The world celebrates Thy birth, O little Babe

of Bethlehem, but I celebrate the birth of the Christ of God in my soul. I commemorate the day when in my consciousness I received the meaning of Thy coming, when I felt my heart throb in answer to Thy call of love.

From one Christmas Eve to the next Christmas Eve I seek to incorporate into my life more of Thy gentleness, more of Thy compassion, more of Thy selflessness, tolerance, and patience toward all. I seek to grow as Thou didst grow, in wisdom and stature and in favor with God and man, that Thy greatness may become my greatness, Thy power for good my power for good, and that I too may become a Christ of God, the Savior of my world.

The star that shone that first Christmas Eve in an age long ago shines as brightly tonight for all whose inner eyes are opened to see the invisible star that heralds the setting up of the Christ kingdom within.

The Christ child is born again in the manger of the heart of everyone who has prepared for His coming, has made room for His entrance through purification, through praise, through faith and expectancy.

The joy of the angels' songs rings as true and

clear this Christmas Eve in the souls of all who
abide in the Christ consciousness, who shepherd
their thoughts, who live in peace and goodwill
toward men, as it did when the angels an-
nounced to the shepherds the birth of the Savior
of the world.

The Wise Men within us are continually
searching the heavens of our consciousness for
the star that proclaims the Christ birth and that
signifies to us the readiness of the soul to receive
their rich gifts.

In my consciousness of unity with Thee, O
omnipresent One, the light of the star shines
in my soul tonight, illumining all the dark
places. The joy of the angels' songs fills my heart
with peace and goodwill to all; the Wise Men
within bring their rich gifts with rejoicing, as
I give all that I am and all that I have to the
Christ of God, born anew in my consciousness
tonight.

Glory to God in the highest! May all persons
come quickly into a consciousness of the Christ
love and goodwill, that there may be between
Him and His children, between country and
country, the peace of God that passeth understanding. Amen! Amen!

The Burden Bearer

O Thou Burden Bearer, how wonderful is Thy promise to all that are weary and heavy laden. When I listen I hear Thee say, "Lo, I am with you always," and I believe. I hear Thee say, "Come unto me" and "Cast all thy burden upon Jehovah," and I accept. Let me feel the fullness of Thy promises. Let me cast all my burdens on Thee, knowing that as I let them go, they are taken up by the One who knows how to make of them the nothingness that they are. Now as I release to Thee all the burdens of my life, I feel my emancipation, my freedom, my lightness. I am emancipated from hard conditions. I am free from doubt and worry; I am lightened of all physical and mental loads. I am a bond servant no longer, but a glorious new creature, spreading my wings to attain new heights of the Christ consciousness.

It is very wonderful, O Christ, to know that Thou who did bear the Cross up Calvary for me are always beside me, Thou who are never weary, never discouraged, never depressed, because Thou knowest the way of life everlasting. It is very wonderful to know that as I look to Thee

and rest in Thee, Thou wilt lift from me every
burden of the day. Through my every Gethsemane, up my every Calvary, through the tomb into
the resurrection Thou art with me, and with
Thee I ascend into a consciousness of spiritual
unity. No longer is the path dark or the burden
heavy, no longer do I grope or sit exhausted by
the way, for Thy presence lights and lifts. Ever in
the consciousness of Thy love and power omnipresent, I am strengthening and renewing my
physical being, and all the affairs of my life are
made successful and easy. In Thee I find rest to
my soul.

Meditation for Wisdom and Guidance

Dear Father, I come to Thee like a little child
not knowing the way. I seek the solution of prob-
lems that I of myself am not able to work out. I
have come to the crossroads and know not the
path to take. I would have guidance beyond the
human that I may make no mistake, that I may
not have to retrace my steps, that I may take the
path that leads to joy for myself and others and
to greater service to Thee. My intellect would

have me go one way, my emotions and desires pull me in another; but I know from past experience that none of these can be relied upon to lead me aright. My faith is not in them; for they do not get their knowledge from Thy omniscience, but depend on people, conditions, and circumstances to give them their leading. My faith is in Thee, O omnipotent God, for in Thee only is the knowledge of the way to right decision.

O Thou omniscient Mind, Thou Knower of all things past, present, and future, make known to me Thy will. It is not my limited will that I would have done, but Thine; for I know that in Thy will for me is all the good that I could desire. Let the angel of Thy presence guide me in a plain path, in a right way, a way that corresponds to Thy will for me. Give me strength and courage to go forward, give me faith to follow, even though there be a cross, even though there be a dark valley before I reach the heights.

O send out Thy light and Thy truth,
Let them lead me,
Let them bring me unto Thy holy hill,
And to Thy tabernacles.

Bedtime Meditation

Father, I thank Thee for the activities of the
day and Thy sustaining strength to complete
them. I thank Thee for the time of rest that
draws near, when I can close the door and draw
the curtain of my mind, shutting out all the
distractions and fascinations of the material
world, and receive undisturbed Thy ministrations, Thine instructions.

Let, O Redeemer, all wrong thoughts of the
day, my thoughts toward others, others'
thoughts toward me, be dissolved in the forgiving love of Jesus Christ. Let all unkind words and
acts be submerged in Thy redeeming grace. Let
all the cares of the day steal away, all anxious
thoughts take flight, as I draw near to Thee, O
Burden Bearer. Let my mind be cleansed of all
error, that I may be pure enough to enter Thy
presence in the hours to come. Let my body relax
so that it may be open enough to receive Thy
spiritual forces, which seek to renew and
strengthen. Let my intellect cease its thoughts so
that my mind may be alert enough to catch Thy
slightest message and to interpret truly all the
dreams and visions of the night. Let this sabbath

of my soul be a time apart with Thee, my Beloved, a time of peace and rest and renewal. Let my soul worship in Thy house, O Lord, and as I behold Thy beauty, let its transforming power find expression in my life, filling all the unlovely places with Thy glory and holiness.

I know that Thou who keep Israel neither slumbers nor sleeps. Because of Thine omnipresence the night shines as the day and Thy song is with me. I will now in faith and peace lay me down to sleep, for Thou, O Father, keep me in safety. The angel of Thine appointing hovers over me so that no harm may come nigh my dwelling. Underneath and around me are the everlasting arms. In Thine omnipresence I rest and rest, and my sleep is sweet.

Meditation for Harmonizing the Elements

Father, I thank Thee for rain in its season, for gentle winds, and merciful clouds, for heat and cold, all adapted by Thy love to meet man's comfort and nature's needs. For all of these Thou has appointed a time so that the beauty and productiveness of Thy creation may increase.

Let nothing hinder the harmony of the whole, but let man and nature work together to restore the perfection of Thy kingdom on earth.

In the beginning the Garden was created for man. He was given it to dress and keep. Power and dominion over all creation was his. He walked and talked with God in the garden of his soul and knew only the good. His world showed forth this peace and harmony of the within. As long as he lived in this relation to his Creator there were no droughts, no floods, no freezing weather, no scorching heat to disturb the beauty of his world. When he began to see good *and* evil, error began to be manifested in his world, and he was in the garden no longer.

Father, all mankind is seeking to return to Thy garden of peace and beauty and plenty. They are seeking their good, which is found only in Thy garden. Let each of Thy children the world over realize that peace must be established in the heart, beauty in the soul, and plenty in the vision, if these are to enter and become manifest in the life. Let us know that we must think thoughts of love and speak words of love, that individual and national clashes must cease, that hatred and cruelty and injustice must be wiped out, that greed and selfishness and jealousy must be overcome, and that the Christ of God must be enthroned in the heart before we can again enter the Garden of Eden.

Father, I thank Thee for Thy love which fills my heart, for Thy wisdom which fills my mind, for Thy clear vision which sees only the good. I claim my birthright of power and dominion, realizing that its foundation is in Thine omnipotence, omniscience, and omnipresence. From this consciousness I now speak peace and harmony to the elements, that all nature may receive direct from Thy hands and fulfill its purpose of beauty and productiveness, in the name and through the power of the One who said to the waves and winds, "Peace, be still," and had instant recognition and obedience. I speak to all Thy creation, "Let the Christ harmony and peace reign supreme in you, that it may be so in the elements."

Meditation for Prosperity

O Thou Giver of gifts, Thou all-inclusive Gift, to Thee I bring my needs, my desires, my limitations, my failures. To my mortal mind they seem great, but to Thine omnipotent Mind they are nothing. I sink my seeing in Thy seeing, and I rest from seeing things or the lack of things. I see only Thee, and Thy beauty and glory and opulence become mine also in mind, body, and affairs. This good which Thou has prepared for me from the beginning, and which continually seeks entrance into my world, makes itself manifest through the door that my faith in Thy love for me has opened.

In the realization of my inheritance I claim the promise that all Thine is mine, and I make Thee, my Father, the promise that all mine is Thine. By this covenant between Thee and me there is opened the channel through which Thy wealth flows to me and out from me, in abundant measure, to bless Thy work and Thy workers. My storehouse and Thy storehouse are full to overflowing, for they are one.

I enter in consciousness the kingdom of God within me, where riches abound. Here I abide, trusting and resting; here I lay up rich treasures of thought that make of me a mighty magnet drawing good into my manifest world. Prosperity flows to me from every direction until "my cup runneth over." As I open my hand, my pocket-book, my bank account, my business, my home to the inflow of Thy substance, each is filled with a prosperity that is eternal, because it comes from Thee who art from everlasting to everlasting. I enter into that peace which brings freedom from anxious thought, because I know in whom I believe, and I know that He who is my supply and my support will never fail me, no matter how great my need may be.

I praise and give thanks to Thee, Thou Giver of gifts, for Thy bountiful substance "pressed out" to me, taking form in whatsoever I need even before the need is manifest, in the ever-overflowing measure of the loaves and fishes, to spare and to share.

The Temple of the Living God

My body, this house which my soul possesses, is the dwelling place of the Most High God. In the holy of holies within my own soul, Spirit waits for me to become conscious of its own in-dwelling perfection, waits for me to cleanse the temple and let spiritual perfection fill my life.

Momentarily, through thought and word and act, I seek to build a body temple so pure, so holy, so harmonious that Spirit may be able to find expression in and through me. I seek to finish with earthiness, that this corruptible may put on the incorruptible, this mortal the immortal, that this flesh may be translated into pure spirit substance, which knows no pain or weakness, no accident or death. I seek to surrender my emotions, my desires to the will of the Highest, that every cell in my body may be resurrected from the deadness that the senses have imposed upon them and become free to express the purity and beauty of Spirit. I seek to find within me the Christ body and to claim it as my own, that the physical may coordinate with the spiritual and become self-renewing, vital, young, beautiful, a redeemed body, formed after the image, patterned after the likeness of the Creator, even the living God.

Thus do I seek to make my body a fit dwelling place for Thee, my beloved, a place in which Thou delightest. Let every thought be as sweet incense on Thine altar, let every word resound as sweet music in a heavenly choir, let kind acts and just deeds form an inner beauty of expression, and that which I am become the holy atmosphere of Thy kingdom.

To Thee, O living God, do I dedicate my body as Thy holy temple. My soul is again at one with Thee in Thy tabernacle, and it is glad. I bid my intellect sit at Thy feet to learn of Thee, that Thy wisdom may be my wisdom and guide my footsteps surely into Thy way of holiness. My eyes I dedicate to the seeing of good only, seeing the Christ in my brother, the Lord in all creation. My ears I dedicate to listening within for Thy message, my mouth to speaking Thy words of Truth. My brain is Thine to use for constructive thinking and lifting of the race consciousness. My hands and feet are to serve Thee and make the path of life more glorious. In all that I do I seek to express Thee.

O living God, take this body temple and let Thy glory express itself in it and through it, that it may be a shining tabernacle through which Thy love and beauty and perfection are shown forth to humankind as our very own.

Meditation for Protection

My heart holds naught but love divine, naught but peace and goodwill. My mind reaches out to bless wherever a blessing may be needed, regardless of creed or race or station. In this consciousness there is no room for antagonism, for contagion, for accidents or terrors, for storms of the elements or emotions. All my world is filled with the harmonizing, uplifting, all-absorbing love of God.

He that keeps me in the hollow of His hand neither slumbers nor sleeps. The angel of His presence wields a flaming sword at the entrance to my world, keeping back all error. The strong right arm of Jehovah God is my defense from all evil. He that keeps me as the apple of His eye makes me to dwell in safety. He keeps my goings-out and comings-in. By day the cloud of His presence hides me from harm, by night the flame of His glory dissolves all the terrors of darkness. In the secret place of the Most High I dwell securely; under the shadow of the Almighty I abide peacefully.

My Father, I give thanks to Thee for the radiance of the Christ presence continually abiding in me. Let whoever crosses my path in hatred, in hardness, in injustice be healed by the image of Thyself radiating through me. Let me be so filled with the Christ love that anyone seeking to enter my world, visibly or invisibly, to harm may become conscious of a love so full, so free, so great that it satisfies him and takes from his heart all error desire. Let him also be lifted up into a realization of his Christ likeness and evermore walk with Thee.

Let me, my Father, feel Thine omnipotence until all the enemies of my household—fear and anxiety, worry and doubt—vanish from my consciousness into utter nothingness to return no more. Let me sit at Thy feet and learn of Thy loving-kindness until love has made friends of all enemies.

To Thee, my Father-God, praise and thanksgiving constantly rise like sweet incense from Thine altar in my heart. For Thine omnipresence continually leading me in paths of righteousness and ways of peace, for Thine omniscience ever before me as a shining light, for Thine omnipotence powerfully dissolving the error, I momently give thanks, my Savior, my Redeemer.

Printed U.S.A.

43-F-8946-7M-8-86

Appendix B

SPIRITUAL REMEDIES FOR PARTICULAR LACKS

[Editor's Note: In 1979 a revised edition of *Effectual Prayer* was published that did not include this section. Concern surrounded how dated some of the entries were and how easy it was to draw the wrong inferences when readers were diagnosing their own symptoms. Both of these concerns remain. In bringing this section back for this Classic Library Series edition, we ask the reader's indulgence. First of all, this listing of "spiritual remedies" is not intended as a substitute for medical treatment, nor should it ever be used in that manner. Second, the last thirty years have indeed demonstrated a powerful connection between the thoughts in our minds and the conditions

in our bodies and life affairs, a connection that
this book and others like it within Unity truly
pioneered. However, this connection is not always as simple and direct as it once appeared.
Many symptoms have multiple causes, with
the mind-body connection playing only a part;
heredity, living conditions, diet, exercise, and
other factors do have a role in health and disease, even if "mind" may be the ultimate cause.
Lastly, prayer and healing affirmations are
clearly proven, powerful healers, but the wise
practitioner will take the aid of all other mo-
dalities that present themselves.

—Michael A. Maday
2000]

EVERY MANIFESTATION of inharmony in
the body and life has its correspondence in the
mind. Either in the conscious mind there are
thoughts not in accord with the law of righteousness—fear, anxiety, intolerance, criticism,
hate, jealousy, lack—or in the subconscious
mind there have in the past been stored away
error thoughts that are as yet unredeemed. In
order to remove the bodily inharmony or the

inharmony in the life we need to counteract
the thought or group of thoughts that is at
the root of the error appearance, and to plant
in this emptied place the good seed of righteous thoughts that will continually increase
and produce in the body and the life that good
only. If thoughts are chosen that are pure truths,
free from intellectual conclusions and deduc-
tions, from emotions and material desires, nothing more is needed except to hold them fast
in the conscious mind until the subconscious
mind grasps them, and the soul realizes its
freedom to express its Christ likeness. Then
does the holy thought come into its own; and
the power of the word being released, it expresses itself first in a consciousness of peace
and harmony, then in a lifting of the feeling
nature into a state of ecstasy or exultation, and
then in a manifestation of peaceful and harmonious living.

All spiritual remedies dissolve errors of consciousness even as a light turned on in a dark
room dissolves the darkness. They bring into
consciousness the light of Truth, even as a lamp
brings light into a darkened room, and the
Truth of life, which is health, joy, abundance,

stands forth even as the true character of the room stands forth when it is revealed by the light. According as we have faith in that which the spiritual remedy expresses—the Truth about ourselves as children and heirs of the Most High God—so Truth will be manifested for us and in us. If our faith is weak and wavering and we keep our vision on the appearance, power is withheld from the words we speak, and the change cannot manifest itself quickly, may never manifest itself; but if our faith is in the Great Physician and we see as already accomplished that which we speak, then the words will be given freedom to express their power and will carry us into the very presence of the divine healer, and our release will be speedy.

The quicker one turns from an appearance of inharmony and dissolves it through the use of a Truth statement, the less hold will it have on the flesh, the less growth will it have in the life. A weed in its early growth is easily pulled up, for it has not yet become firmly established; but the longer it remains, the further out and deeper down does it send its roots, making it harder to uproot and causing a greater disturbance to the soil and surrounding plants. To take at once, when errors are felt or seen, a statement of Truth that denies the cause of the appearance and affirms its opposite, the spiritual reality, is to enter quickly the realm of the pattern in the Mount, from which comes perfect expression. Thus there is wiped out root and branch, through contact with the Father within who doeth the works, that which causes the discord in the life, and it is mastered or controlled before it has spread to other parts of the outer expression.

A human being has the will to use, the power to choose, one of two ways of thought activity, either the Adamic consciousness of mixed good and evil or the pure Christ consciousness of the spiritual reality. Only that which is "very good" is of God's creation and worthy of our consideration, our acceptance of anything less than this puts us under bondage to sense consciousness. To co-operate with the Creator in His "very good" is to recognize the divinity of the Self, the diseaseless, deathless, sinless Self, the triumphant Son of God with power and dominion over all error; and to recognize this is to open the way for its manifestation in reality.

The spiritual "remedies" outlined here have
been given the writer in answer to a call on
the omniscient Mind for the highest help avail-
able for others in their time of need, in cleansing, renewing, and making them harmonious
according to the perfect pattern. They are to be
used to deny the root cause of the inharmony
of the body or life, thus cleansing the mental
realm, and then to lift the mind to the purity
and faith of the Christ. They are to be used to
deny the line of thought that has caused the
error appearance and to affirm the spiritual reality needed to counteract it and to build in
that which the discordant thought has hidden
for the time being. Thus does one enter the
realm from which Jesus Christ functioned when
He spoke forgiveness of sins; when He made
the deaf to hear, the dumb to speak, the lame
to walk, the blind to see; when He restored
the fevered body, and raised up the dead into
new and vital living. In this state of consciousness, all things are possible and nothing is
hard, because one has lost consciousness of the
weak and limited personal self and become one
with the miracle-working Christ of God. He
who said, "Come unto me, all ye that labour

and are heavy laden," has been given the burden of circumstances or conditions, and you find rest unto soul and body when He enters and does His perfect work.

The spiritual remedies given here state the Truth, no matter what the appearance may be, no matter what the senses claim, no matter what others say. Accept them in faith as from the Great Physician. Take the prayer that fits your need. Repeat it over and over until it is fixed in your conscious mind. Repeat it yet over and over until your whole being recognizes that it is the Truth concerning the Self, until the very flesh vibrates to the words. Then drop the denial portion of the prayer and hold the affirmation until it continues to say itself subconsciously when you are about the day's duties or asleep in your bed at night. Then you will find the power of the word becoming flesh to dwell with you, expressing itself in joy and beauty, in wholeness and plenty.

As we continually turn to the spiritual remedy to meet each situation in our lives, we will find growing in us a fuller consciousness of the one Presence and one Power omnipresent in our lives. As we keep the high watch, turn-

ing always in faith toward the Giver of gifts,
claiming the Truth about ourselves as children
and heirs of God, we will find our inheritance
in what the Father is and in what the Father
has becoming manifest here and now. As we
look away from every error appearance, from
pain and ache and disease, to the perfect Christ
body within, bone of His bone, flesh of His
flesh, the very life and substance of His being,
we will find purity and perfection manifesting itself in our body temples, and we will
become new creatures in Christ Jesus, every whit
whole. Then will we come into that which mortal eye hath not seen, nor physical ear heard,
neither the intellect conceived; we will come
into a consciousness of the glory that our souls
had with the Father in the beginning, when we
were the delight of the Creator, master workers with Him in creating the good. Beloved,
may this be your experience through the use
of the words given by the omniscient Mind to
one whose whole desire in life is to be of service in lifting humanity out of suffering and
sorrow, poverty and death into its divine inheritance of peace and beauty, joy and plenty,
glorious living here and now.

A Daily Self-Treatment

There is within me the perfect pattern of a perfect body, even the Christ body. I constantly turn my vision to this body, and that which it expresses in and through me makes perfect this temple of the living God. In accordance with the pattern, my body is strong, vital, alive all over, diseaseless and incorruptible, eternally young and beautiful. Every cell is illumined by the Christ life within. Every organ is constantly renewing and functioning in spiritual perfection. Every gland is performing that for which it was created. The life stream flows peacefully through me, cleansing and renewing. The breath of God in me makes me alive all over. My whole body coordinates with the Christ body to bring its inner beauty and perfection into expression.

Now, today, I express my God-given right of power and dominion over all that opposes spiritual perfection. Divine love and wisdom guide my every thought and word and act. My dependence is altogether on the omniscient, omnipotent, omnipresent Christ of God in me, and everything that I undertake is blessed into expressing exceeding great good.

I thank Thee, Father-Mother God, that Thou hast placed in me the perfect Christ pattern, together with the power to bring it into perfect expression for my joyful use and Thy service. Let me express it always according to Thy highest thought of me. Let me come again into a conscious union with Thee. Thine is the power and the glory forever.

Adenoids

Child of God, no personality can limit you, restrict you; no thought in the race consciousness can obstruct the purpose for which you came into being. You are free to express your perfect Self now. Freely and fully you breathe in and breathe out the life and breath of God, and every part of your being is cleansed, vitalized, renewed, and made completely whole. "Suffer little children, and forbid them not, to come unto me."

Anemia

I erase from my consciousness all thoughts of lack, all fears of not having enough, all claims of disease, all pernicious thoughts of limitation. Gone are they into the nothingness from which they came. God is my life, my supply, my all in all, and His love for me expresses itself as health and strength, as wisdom and guidance, as success and prosperity. Utterly I trust my Father-God to supply from His rich substance every need of my body, every need of my life. "In him we live, and move, and have our being."

Appendicitis

Through the love of God in me, my mind is purged of all irritable thoughts, all inflamed thoughts. I release all congested thoughts. I erase all unjust thoughts. There is nothing in me that withholds compassion from any of God's creation. Every part of my being is open and receptive to the cleansing, free-flowing life of Spirit; and filled with this life, I am renewed according to the perfect God pattern. I am whole, praise God. "God is love; and he that abideth in love abideth in God, and God abideth in him."

Asthma

I release from my consciousness all thoughts of fear, of suppression, of limitation. I declare

my freedom from conditions, from materiality, from the race consciousness of error.

God is my life, and there is nothing else in
my life before Him. "The breath of the Almighty,"
which is without beginning or end, fills my
nostrils as a cleansing, vitalizing force that re-
creates my whole organism, until I again express myself in His perfect image and likeness.
"The Spirit of God hath made me, / And the
breath of the Almighty giveth me life."

Arteries

I do not believe in old age, in the lessening of mental and physical powers as the years
pass. I do not believe in hard conditions, in
luck, in chance. I am not hard in my dealings
with others, but seek to show the compassion
that I would myself receive. The river of life
flows from the throne of God in my heart into
every vein and capillary and artery in my body,
keeping them clean and vital, and daily they
perform their prescribed purpose in keeping
young and perfect this temple of the living
God. "In thy presence is fulness of joy; in thy
right hand there are pleasures for evermore."

Bladder

There is no weakness, no inflammation, in any part of my body, for my body is not just flesh and blood; it is Spirit. Every organ and every function in me is doing its work in divine order, according to the purpose for which it was created, and I am eternally strong, harmonious, alive in Christ. I express my perfect Self now. "I will give unto him that is athirst of the fountain of the water of life freely."

Blood, Cleansing of

I am forgiven and cleansed, both consciously and subconsciously, of all impurity of thought. The holiness of the Christ Mind in me purifies and vitalizes my blood, and it flows freely, a cleansing, healing stream of life, nourishing, upbuilding, and renewing me in every part of my being, and I am whole. "Behold, I make all things new."

Blood Poisoning

No poison or infection can drink up the Spirit of life in me, neither can my life be lessened. The pure water of the river of life flows fully and freely into every cell in my body, cleansing, healing, vitalizing, and restoring me to the perfect likeness of my Creator. "The law of the Spirit of life in Christ Jesus made me free from the law of sin and of death."

Blood Pressure, High

I relax and let go of all life's tensions and anxieties. I take firm hold of my Father-God and enter into such complete rest in Him that all the thoughts of my mind, the functions of my body, and the affairs of my life become divinely ordered. "I will never leave thee, nor forsake thee."

Boils

The love of Christ in me wipes from my mind all impure states, all angry, boiling-over thoughts. Pure Spirit substance fills me through and through, and my flesh becomes as the flesh of a little child, free from spot and blemish and shining with beauty and purity. "Let the word of Christ dwell in you richly; in all wisdom."

Bones, Broken, Diseased

No part of the temple of the living God, which my body is, can be broken or diseased or inharmonious. I submit my body to the Creator, who is able to heal, to adjust, to restore me to the image and likeness of Himself. Now am I perfectly whole in every part, praise God: "I in them, and thou in me, that they may be perfected into one."

Bronchitis

Every trace and taint of error is wiped from my mind and body. My breath is continually one with and inseparable from the breath of God. I am made free and whole in the name and through the power of the Christ of God, ever present in my soul. God "giveth to all life, and breath, and all things."

Burns; Bruises

Flesh in itself has no consciousness of pain, neither does the Spirit of life in me suffer; therefore, I am freed forever. I am immersed in the soothing, healing, harmonizing balm of the Christ presence, and my flesh exultantly turns to its Creator and is made perfect and whole. "He hath clothed me with the garments of salvation, he hath covered me with the robe of righteousness."

Cancer

There is no grief or resentment hidden within me to eat away my peace of mind. I forgive and am forgiven, and no longer does my heart hold less than God's good. A healing flame of divine love wipes clean every cell in my body, and the rich substance of Spirit renews, vitalizes, and makes me whole in every part. The Christ body takes full possession of my flesh body, and I am restored to the image and likeness of my Creator, praise God! "All things are possible to him that believeth."

Catarrh

No thoughts of impurity concerning myself or another can dwell in the pure realm of Spirit that is within me. I am clean and whole through and through, for each cell in the mucous membrane of my body is filled with the purifying, vitalizing life and substance of Spirit.

"Let the words of my mouth and the meditation of my heart / Be acceptable in thy sight, / O Jehovah, my rock, and my redeemer."

Change of Life

There is no change of life in my consciousness, for I know that life is from everlasting to everlasting, and of God, who is eternal and changeless. I am filled with omnipresent life in its divine completeness, and it is continually cleansing, renewing, strengthening, and forming every part of my body into the Christ image. I am eternally young in my likeness to God my Father, and nothing can take from me my divine inheritance of perfection. "Let thy lovingkindness and thy truth continually preserve me."

Circulation

I am cleansed of every unholy thought that would cause a break in my unity with God. The stream of life flows in an unending, unbroken circle in me, nourishing, upbuilding, and renewing my body, and I am whole, complete now. "I and the Father are one."

Colds

I erase from my mind all negativeness, that I may become one with the positiveness of Being. I erase from my body all tenseness, that it may receive the healing current. I enter the stream of God's quickening, renewing life. It flows fully and freely into every cell of my being, and I am strengthened, harmonized, vitalized, and made every whit whole. "My grace is sufficient for thee: for *my* power is made perfect in weakness."

Constipation

I let go in my mind, releasing to Christ my Saviour, the affairs of my life, and I trust Him fully to regulate them all. In Him all tensing thoughts and their resultant conditions pass from me, and the elimination of all error from mind and body is complete. The free-flowing love of God establishes law and order in me, and every function of my body performs its perfect work. I praise God that now is my whole being released from bondage and lifted up to everlasting freedom of expression. "Ye shall know the truth, and the truth shall make you free."

Corns, Calluses

There is nothing in me to harden the flesh of my body. The love of God in me erases from my consciousness every hard thought I have ever entertained toward people or conditions. The Christ who dwelleth in me is adjusting and correcting and bringing into its original purity and perfection every cell of my flesh. The joy of the Lord fills me, my mind, body, and affairs. "I . . . cause those that love me to inherit substance, / And . . . I may fill their treasuries."

Danger

I fear no evil, no accident, for Thou, O Christ, art within me, around me, above me, below me to guard, to guide, and to lead me in paths of pleasantness and ways of peace. "Greater is he that is in you than he that is in the world."

Deafness

I cease to close myself to the will of the Highest for me. I cease to be rebellious as regards circumstances and conditions. I open my inner ear to the voice of my indwelling Christ that I may be guided in the ways of righteousness. I am alert, ready, willing to be used. I am obedient to the Christ message, and the miracle-working power of the omnipresent Christ touches every dark and inactive cell in my ears, and they are resurrected into livingness, made every whit whole. I hear, I hear, praise God. "Great and marvelous are thy works, O Lord God."

Debt

I wipe from my consciousness every thought of another person's debt to me, for I hold anyone who owes me a debt in the thought of God's rich abundance and justice. My consciousness of obligation is to love God and my fellow humans, and in living according to this consciousness, I wipe out from my life every other obligation. I am free, successful, prospered. I give joyously the tithe of all that I earn to the Giver of gifts, and He opens the doors of His rich storehouse and pours out His good to me in His good measure, pressed together, shaken down, and running over. "Jehovah will . . . bless all the work of thy hand, and thou shalt lend into many nations, and thou shalt not borrow."

Despondency; Depression

I will not let downward thought control my mind. I am strong in the Lord, and the power of His might brings to me a full-rounded life of joyful experience. The indwelling Christ, to whom I intrust all my affairs, leads me to express His glory in my body, and makes me successful in all that I undertake, even to demonstrating the Father's overflowing measure of rich living. I am poised and balanced in Spirit, and nothing can move me from my faith in my own lordship to guide me and guard me and give me love and wisdom to express the law of righteousness in all my activities. "Cast thy burden upon Jehovah, and he will sustain thee: / He will never suffer the righteous to be moved."

Diarrhea

I do not waste myself in riotous living or in thought or in emotion or in material self-seeking. I do not allow unkind thoughts to dwell in my mental realm or take form in my actions. I put my whole being, mind, body, and affairs under the control of the all-powerful

Christ Mind in me, and every part of my body functions in divine order and harmony. I am cleansed, healed, renewed, made every whit whole in mind and body, praise be to God. "The prayer of faith shall save him that is sick, and the Lord shall raise him up."

Dizziness

I refuse to let my sensual nature deviate me from the path of Truth. I am one with absolute Principle, in which there is no variation, neither shadow of turning. God is the one presence and one power in my life. I keep my vision fixed steadfastly on Him, and I am continually poised and balanced in all the activities of mind, body, and affairs. "God . . . girdeth me with strength, / And maketh my way perfect."

Drug Habit; Drunkenness

I am no longer bound by sense pleasure and false appetite. My satisfaction is in Christ my Saviour, and in Him I am made strong, peaceful, powerful. Ever beside me stands my Lord Christ, giving me courage and self-mastery. Through Him I am lifted up into joyous freedom and righteous living, and I am forever satisfied. "Sin shall not have dominion over you: for ye are not under law, but under grace."

Earache

I am not resistant, rebellious, obstinate. I am the willing, obedient child of my Father-God, and I co-operate with Him in bringing only the good into expression. The soothing power of the Holy Spirit infolds me and fills me. My mind is filled with peace and good-will, and my body now expresses complete ease and harmony. "Draw nigh to God, and he will draw nigh to you."

Ear Noise

There is no confusion in my mind, no perplexity, no resistance to conditions. All fear and unrest and resentment have departed far from me. I am ready and willing for the will of God to be done in me and through me. I put my trust in God my Father, and I listen deep within for His guidance, and Him only do I follow. Now is peace and harmony established in my ears, for the still small voice within speaks: "Peace, be still." "The God of

peace make you perfect in every good thing
to do His will."

Eczema

All spots and all blemishes are removed from
my body, for every cell of my skin is filled with
the life and substance of Spirit. I am made
strong in my Christ likeness, and my body radiates His indwelling presence. "In my flesh
shall I see God."

Epilepsy

No longer can my sensual nature hold me
in its desires. I am purified and vitalized, I
am upheld and made free by the consciousness
of the Christ of God in my soul. The body is
obedient to the heavenly vision, and forever
am I pure, strong, steady, whole. "Is anything
too hard for Jehovah?"

Eye Challenges

I do not indulge in downward visioning. I
do not see as real the appearances. I join my
vision with the God vision that is too pure to
behold iniquity. I see near, and I see far; I see

all things in purity and clearness, for I see with the eyes of Spirit. "If . . . thine eye be single [seeing good only], thy whole body shall be full of light."

Failure

God cannot fail; therefore, as His son I cannot fail. I am strong, steady, wise, poised in God-Mind, which is omniscient, omnipotent, omnipresent; and in this Mind I know all things and can do all things. Through Christ, who strengthens me, I am led into my own good and am prospered and successful in its doing. I thank God for success, glorious success, in carrying out that which He has given me to do. "For it is God that worketh in you both to will and to do of His good pleasure."

Fainting, Prevention of

Nothing within or without can disturb my equilibrium. I am one with God almightiness, and in Him I am poised and balanced. I shall not be fainthearted before conditions and circumstances, for my heart is courageous and fearless. I am one with the Christ, and His strength and power uphold me. "The eternal God is thy dwelling place, / And underneath are the everlasting arms."

Falling

I do not submit to failure. I do not let emotions overwhelm me. I am upright in all my dealings. I am poised and balanced in Spirit. Spirit is like an iron rod in the midst of me, and I cannot be moved from the Truth of my being. The angel of His presence has been given charge over me to bear me up in His hands lest I dash my foot against a stone. "Underneath are the everlasting arms."

Fear

I am not apprehensive of evil; I do not let fearful emotions drive me. I am consciously in the midst of Omnipresence, where nothing of an error nature can enter. The Christ of God dwelling in me guides me and guards me and protects me. "Thou wilt keep him in perfect peace, whose mind is stayed on thee: because he trusteth in thee."

Fevers

I am not held in the mortal belief of contagion, weakness. I do not give power to germs, to disease. I am bold and courageous, because my Father-God holds me in the hollow of His hand. My flesh rests in peace, for every atom of my being is cleansed, healed, renewed by the miracle-working power of Jehovah God, which has touched me—soul, mind, and body— into ever-lasting newness. "Let patience have its perfect work, that ye may be perfect and entire, lacking nothing."

Foot Challenges

I do not believe that the path of life is a hard and weary way to travel. I know that my Redeemer liveth and ever maketh intercession for me; therefore, my path is pleasant and my way is peace. My feet are firmly established on the rock of Thy covenant, O God, and each day Thou dost make more perfect my understanding of Thy law. "Thy word is a lamp unto my feet, / And a light unto my path."

Forgiveness

Consciously and subconsciously I am cleansed from anger, malice, hatred, and grudges through the forgiving love of Jesus Christ, who gave Himself that His consciousness might be mine also. I am such a radiant center of love that every error in me is wiped out, and every error thought directed toward me is baptized with the Christ love and its owner set free. I, too, am free, and with the Christ in me, I say to everything and everybody: "God bless you! I love you and forgive you." "Love worketh no ill to his neighbor: love therefore is the fulfillment of the law."

Gallstones

I let no thoughts of hardness fill my heart, nor do I let grief make hardened conditions in my body consciousness. The oil of joy hath been given me for mourning, and I open myself fully to this cleansing, renewing stream of life. The Word that was made flesh dwells within me, and my flesh becomes glorified in His presence. I am healed in mind and body now, and my soul rejoices in its freedom of expression. "I am Jehovah thy God, the Holy One of Israel, thy Saviour."

Germs

In God's atmosphere, in which I live and move and have my being, there is nothing but life activity. I am established in Omnipresence and am kept as the apple of His eye. No harm shall come nigh my dwelling. "A thousand shall fall at thy side, / And ten thousand at thy right hand; / But it shall not come nigh thee."

Glands

There is no part of my being—soul, mind, body—closed to the work for which it was created. Unhindered, freely, and fully the stream of God life flows through me, and every function of my body now performs in divine order and harmony. "The word of Christ dwell in you richly."

Goiter; Hyperthyroidism

I let go of all grasping thoughts; I cease reaching out for the fulfillment of my desires. I look to the indwelling Christ for every need of my life, and I find complete satisfaction. Thy power, O Christ, Thy wisdom and love are expressed through me and for me and from me, and I am restored to the glory I had with Thee in the beginning. "The Father abiding in me doeth his works."

Grippe; Influenza

Negativeness cannot grip me and fear cannot hold me, for I am established in the all-powerful life of Jesus Christ. In Him I am made strong and harmonious, in Him I am made alive through and through, and I am now lifted up in a perfect expression of His wholeness and purity. "Behold thou art made whole."

Hair, Treatment for

There is no lack of life or strength in any part of my body. The renewing, restoring, vitalizing life of Spirit fills every cell in me, and the hair of my head is now made perfect in quality and in quantity. "Ye are complete in him."

Hands, Treatment for

My hands are not restless, neither are they idle. They are folded often in prayer, and the God of my salvation fills them with His life and abundance. I give my hands utterly to execute Thy love and mercy, O Christ, and Thou dost bless them and make them profitable unto Thee and Thy creation. "My soul, wait thou in silence for God only; / For my expectation is from him."

Hay Fever

Every error of every day of the past is washed from my consciousness and has been stripped of all power of recurrence. I live today in the glorious presence of the Son of God, and my whole being is filled with His purifying, vitalizing, strengthening life. I know the Truth of my being, and I am free, praise God. "The law of the Spirit of life in Christ Jesus made me free from the law of sin and of death."

Headache

I am not bound in flesh ways, neither do I entertain thoughts of fear and worry that disturb my mental realm. In God is my supply, my health, my satisfaction. From head to foot, I am filled with the Christ life that makes me whole, free, alive all over. "Thou hast anointed my head with oil; / My cup runneth over."

Heart Challenges

No longer do I allow fear, weakness, impurity of thought, hatred, or unforgiveness to find lodgement in my heart. I look to the Christ who dwelleth in me, to lead me and guide me. Every cell and muscle, every valve and nerve of my heart is under the control of the river of life that flows from the throne of God in my heart. My heart beats in unison with the great heart of the universe, and I am at peace within and without. "Search me, O God, and know my heart: / Try me, and know my thoughts; / And see if there be any wicked way in me, / And lead me in the way everlasting."

Hemorrhage

I do not believe in losses of any kind. I do not waste myself in mind or body. All the issues of my life are from God, and the stream of His life flows in an unbroken circle within me. "My life is hid with Christ in God."

Hemorrhoids

My body is not material. It is spiritual, and my flesh manifests the purity and wholeness of Spirit. The free-flowing life of the Holy Spirit expresses itself in and through me, freeing me from all bondage to aches and pains, and I am whole now within and without. "Set your mind on the things that are above, not on the things that are upon the earth."

Hysteria

I am not affected by every wind that blows, by people's acts and opinions. I am not anxious and fearful. I claim my birthright of power and dominion, and the Christ within me sustains and strengthens me in all the activities of my life. I am poised and balanced now in the omniscient, omnipotent God of my being. "The beloved of Jehovah shall dwell in safety by him; / He covereth him all the day long."

Indigestion

I no longer seek to live by bread alone, but I trust the Word of God in me to sustain and strengthen me. I do not worry and fret over circumstances and conditions, but I lift my vision to the Burden Bearer and am free. I release my stomach from all thoughts of inactivity and weakness, and the intelligence in every cell works to establish harmony and perfection. Divine wisdom in me selects my food and uses it to nourish and upbuild my body temple. I thank Thee, Father, for the life and substance of the Christ body, which fills me and makes this body a fit dwelling place for Thy holy Spirit, a body pure, young, beautiful, daily renewed according to the pattern in the Mount. "O taste and see that the Lord is good: blessed is the man that trusteth in him."

Inflammation

I do not allow emotions to control me. I will not allow anger and indignation to get the better of me. My mind is filled with peace and love, which are reflected in my body as purity and wholeness. Forever am I free from that which inflames the flesh; for I give myself to the blessedness of the Christ consciousness that is in me, too pure to behold iniquity. "The fruit of the Spirit are love, joy, peace, long-suffering, kindness, goodness, faithfulness, meekness, self-control; against such there is no law."

Influenza

I will not entertain fear of any kind in my thought world. I put negativeness far from me. Resting in the knowledge of the infolding love of God, I know that every cell and organ of my body is filled with the vitalizing, free-flowing life of Spirit. Now am I raised up in new life, strong, vital, fearless, whole. "There shall no evil befall thee, / Neither shall any plague come nigh thy tent."

Inheritance

I can inherit nothing of error, because I am a child of God. My birthright is power and dominion over all lesser creations. My inheritance is God's "very good." I am made in His image, after His likeness, and I express now and forever the Christ purity and wholeness, the Christ success and abundance given me by my Father-Mother God. "The Spirit himself beareth witness with our spirit, that we are children of God."

Insanity

There is no darkness, no dimness of perception in you, for Christ is your eternal light. You are no longer held in bondage by error thoughts, vain imaginings, but are loosed and free with the freedom of Spirit. The Christ of God in you controls your every thought and word and act; and soul, mind, and body coordinate to express your spiritual perfection. Now are you free, the child of God, triumphant over error. "If any man is in Christ, he is a new creature: the old things are passed away; behold they are become new."

Injustice

My mind is freed from all unjust thoughts toward others, and all the acts of my life express divine love and justice. I am returned full and just compensation, in running-over measure in all my affairs. "Let us not be weary in well-doing: for in due season we shall reap, if we faint not."

Insomnia

No fearful or anxious thought can disturb my peace of mind, for I put myself in the care of God, my Father. I am clothed safely round with the loving care of the Father for His child. In His presence and in communion with Him in my soul, I relax and let go of all nervousness, and I rest and rest and rest and rest. "In peace will I both lay me down and sleep; / For thou, Jehovah alone makest me dwell in safety."

Joints, Stiff

I erase from my mind all thoughts of criticism, all bitterness, unforgiveness, false pride. I establish the joy of the Lord in my mind and let it flow freely through my being, lubricating my joints, freeing my movements, and putting gladness into my life. I praise God for His oil of joy, which finds expression in me and through me and for me in His overflowing measure. "I rejoice always; pray without ceasing; in everything give thanks."

Kidney Trouble

I do not fear disease, old age, failure, poverty. They have no place in my mind or life, because I am eternally one with the Christ who maketh all things new and according to the perfect pattern. All the cells in my kidneys are in divine order and harmony, performing the functions for which they were created. I am alive and radiant in the life of the Spirit. "I will take sickness away from the midst of thee."

Lack

There is no lack in my life, for I have found the riches of my Father's heavenly kingdom within myself. Within myself, I contact God's invisible substance, and it fulfills the purpose for which it was created in supplying me with its overflowing abundance. I am one with God and with His everlasting, inexhaustible, and eternal substance, and the treasury of my inheritance is manifest now: "Give, and it shall be given unto you; good measure, pressed down, shaken together, running over."

Liver Challenges

Criticism and condemnation have no place in my consciousness. I judge not according to appearances, but judge righteous judgment. I am filled and thrilled with infinite love and lifted up into the joy of my Lord Christ. Spirit penetrates and interpenetrates every cell in my liver, freeing it to the healthful activity of the divine purpose. Now am I whole, pure, alive. "With what measure ye mete, it shall be measured to you again."

Losses

Spirit cannot suffer losses, and I take my true place in Spirit. My body is one with the Christ body and cannot lose the beauty and youth and wholeness of Spirit. My supply comes from the Lord, my banker, and can never be diminished. No body and no thing can take from me that which is my divine inheritance, for there was prepared in the beginning enough for all of God's creation. We each claim our own and are satisfied. "Jehovah is a sun and a shield: / Jehovah will give grace and glory; /

No good thing will he withhold from them that walk uprightly."

Lungs, Treatment for

No part of my body is closed to the free-flowing life of Spirit. I breathe in and I breathe out the breath of God, and His livingness fills every cell of my lungs, expanding them in purity, strength, and wholeness. "[Jesus] breathed on them, and said unto them, Receive ye the Holy Spirit."

Malaria

No climate or condition can affect the purity of my mental realm and body consciousness. I am free with the freedom of Spirit, and the life of God in me resurrects every cell that is in darkness in its true livingness. Now am I strong and whole, alive through and through. "Then shall thy light break forth as the morning, and thy healing shall spring forth speedily."

Menses

I am not held in bondage by pain or depression. Every atom of weakness and impurity is washed from mind and body. I am one with the pure life of Spirit. Divine order and harmony are established in every part of my body temple, and every organ and function is performing its purpose in perfection and peace. "Jehovah is the strength of my life."

Nervous Breakdown

I put from my mind all thoughts of hard work, overwork, and injustice, as well as all fears of limitation; Spirit can never be exhausted in strength or supply, and I now claim my oneness with Spirit. I open myself to the free-flowing life of Spirit, and every nerve in my body receives the soothing, healing, harmonizing, inexhaustible life of Spirit. I am strengthened, vitalized, and made whole now by the miracle-working power dwelling within my own soul. "The Lord . . . in the midst of thee is mighty; he wilt save, He will rejoice over thee . . . with singing."

Nervousness

I let nothing within or without disturb my peace of mind. I am at peace with God and my neighbor. The love of God fills me, upholds me, guards and guides me, and I trust

Him utterly with all the affairs of my life. I relax in this knowledge and let His soothing, harmonizing love make my nerves strong and whole. "Thou wilt keep *him* in perfect peace, *whose* mind is stayed on *thee;* because he trusteth in thee."

Neuralgia; Neuritis

I do not allow thoughts of lack and limitation to tear down the vitality of my body. I do not worry or carry in my mind anxious thoughts concerning tomorrow. Steadfastly I face God, my Father, and trust Him to supply every need of my life. The soothing, harmonizing, free-flowing life of the Holy Spirit touches every cell in my body, and I am made peaceful and perfect in my flesh now. "Thou openest thy hand, / And satisfiest the desire of every living thing."

Obesity

I let go of grasping thoughts. I cease clinging to materiality, losses, thoughts of accumulation, that the righteous law of giving and receiving may be equalized in my body and affairs. I look unto Thee, O God, and seeing the

harmony and balance of Thy spirit, I am lightened of superfluous materiality and also become harmonious and balanced in Thee. I trust
the Father who knoweth my needs to provide
for me richly even before the need is manifest.
I look unto Thee, O God, and am lightened.
"I will behold thy face in righteousness: I shall
be satisfied, when I awake, with thy likeness."

Obsession

I do not allow morbid thoughts or dominat-
ing personalities to control me. There is but
one Presence and one Power in my life, and
in this presence and power I am free, strong,
courageous. Now do I claim my Christ likeness, and my whole world expresses this rulership in my mind, which radiates in glorious
living. "Lo, I am with you always."

Old Age

I do not believe in old age, limitation, failure, death. Momently do I renew all the fac-
ulties of mind and body in the allness of Spirit;
and my mind is alert and wise, my body is
strong, supple, fresh, beautiful, young. Every
function of my body, in touch with its coun-

terpart in the Christ body, constantly renews itself unto perfection; every cell in me is given the power to create harmony and order in the body, and the life and substance of Spirit fill me through and through. I have perpetual youth in Christ. I am one with His body, expressing His perfection. "In him we live, and move, and have our being."

Pain

My body cannot suffer from conflict or distress, for I now claim for it harmonious, perfect expression from this unity with its Creator. I open my body consciousness to the peaceful, harmonious expression of Spirit, and my flesh is soothed and made quiet in every part now. God's will for me is peace, and resting in His will for me, I am satisfied. "My presence shall go with thee, and I will give thee rest."

Palsy

No longer can my own fears or the fears of the race consciousness master me. My subconscious mind is cleansed from past human failures and weakness. The Christ of God dwells continually in me, holding me firm and steady in my consciousness of divinity, and my body is now poised and strong, filled with energy and vitality, fitted to serve the Spirit in rich livingness. "God hath not given us the spirit of fear; but of power, and of love, and of a sound mind."

Paralysis

There is no lack of life anywhere in my body, for the activity of Spirit is complete in me, restoring me to my original perfection in God-Mind. Now am I resurrected in every cell of my body into vital livingness, a new creature in Christ Jesus, alive and harmonious in mind and body: free, thank God. "It is the spirit that giveth life."

Piles; Hemorrhoids

I am not sensitive, neither do I let others' acts and opinions disturb my mental world. I stand with my indwelling Christ, and the purity and power of His presence in me cleanses and restores to perfection every cell in my body. "In God have I put my trust, / I will not be afraid; / What can man do unto me?"

Pleurisy; Pneumonia

Mortal thoughts cannot bind free Spirit in me. I am one with and immersed in the almighty stream of God-life, and its cleansing, renewing power restores me to wholeness. I breathe in and breathe out the breath of God, and I become a living soul again, expressing my birthright to perfection. "Be filled with the Spirit."

Poisons

Nothing of a material nature can in any way harm Spirit, which is my real nature. The life and substance of the Christ body fill me to the exclusion of all unlike it. Now am I one with the Father within, who doeth the works, and my body temple is now made perfect and pure, a holy (whole) expression of His love. "Behold, I have given you authority to tread upon serpents and scorpions, and over all the power of the enemy: and nothing shall in any wise hurt you."

Poverty

I do not believe in lack, limitation, poverty, or failure and will not for one moment allow such thoughts to enter my consciousness. I fill my mind to overflowing with rich thoughts, success thoughts, and they take form in my life. I am the son of a King, rich beyond comparison, and all that the Father hath is mine. Now do I claim all that I need and desire in that running-over measure which implies enough and to spare and share. I claim and have my own, that which the Creator prepared for me in the beginning, and I praise and give thanks for its manifestation as plenty, plenty, plenty. "They that seek Jehovah shall not want any good thing."

Prolapsus; "Fallen" Conditions

No part of my body is "fallen" or can fall from its rightful position in the Christ body, for I claim now my likeness to my Creator, expressing it in harmony and order. I look up unto Thee, O great Burden Bearer, and Thou dost make easy and light the burdens of the day. Omniscient, omnipotent One, in Thee I am lifted up into a glorious expression of Thyself. I praise and give thanks continuously for the gladness of living in Thee. "I, if I be lifted up from the earth, will draw all men unto myself."

Proud Flesh; Ulcer

Nothing can become manifest in my body but that which is of my spiritual nature, for I claim my perfection as a child of God. The quick-flowing, cleansing life of Spirit expresses itself in my flesh, and it is restored to spiritual purity and wholeness. My flesh rests in peace. "We look not at the things which are seen, but at the things which are not seen."

Pyorrhea; Gingivitis

I cleanse my mind of all negativeness, of doubts and fears, of all thoughts that do not measure up to the purity of the Christ standard. I establish myself in the all-powerful mind of God, and my flesh is obedient to the heavenly vision. God-life is purifying and vitalizing every cell in my mouth, and my gums and teeth are renewed and made perfect in the pure life and substance of Spirit. "Jesus Christ healeth thee."

Rental or Sale of Property

I look not out for help in my need; I look within to God for the fulfillment of my desires.

Now do I place this property that Thou hast given to me in Thy omniscient Mind, and Thou who knowest all things dost draw to me the one whose need will be fulfilled in the filling of my need. I thank Thee, Father, that in Thy love Thou hast blessed me and prospered me, and that Thou wilt bless and prosper the next occupant of this property, which I have through Thee released fully. Let justice rule in each of our hearts and be carried out in our deeds. "No good thing will he withhold from them that walk uprightly."

Rheumatism; Arthritis

I let no thoughts of anxiety, criticism, or condemnation fill my thought world. No sharp and biting words will I speak to hurt others. I will continuously lift my vision past human frailty to Christ my Saviour, and His forgiving love and compassion transform me into His likeness. Now am I made glad in the strong, vital expression of my body, through the stream of love soothingly encompassing and filling and renewing me. "Give diligence to present thyself approved unto God, a workman that needeth not to be ashamed, handling aright the word of truth."

Rupture

No longer do I allow thoughts of separation of myself and my good to alienate me from my complete life in Christ. I give myself fully to Spirit, and Spirit is quick and active in me to make me one and complete in itself. The Creator's idea of me is now made perfect in my mind and body, and I am strong, steady, pure, whole. "In Him [Christ] dwelleth all the fulness of the Godhead bodily. And ye are complete in him."

Skin Challenges

I look to the Christ of God to wipe from my consciousness all eruptive, impure, inharmonious thoughts, and to sustain me in purity and harmony. I make union with the life and substance of Spirit, and my flesh becomes as a little child's—pure, spotless, beautiful, radiant with life. "They that are wise shall shine as the brightness of the firmament."

Spinal Trouble

There is no weakness in Spirit, and I am Spirit. I claim my birthright to spiritual and physical perfection, for I am a child of God. In this realization of my inheritance of perfection, I am strong, upright, vital, alive through and through. The Tree of Life in the midst of me bears its fruits of love and peace and purity, and my physical body is renewed according to this pattern, expressing the glorious life of the Christ body. "I am Jehovah that healeth thee." "I will take sickness away from the midst of thee."

Solar Plexus, Treatment for

There is no darkness in my body temple, for in the midst of me is the light that lighteth every man that cometh into the world. Every dark and inactive cell in my body is filled with the glory of the Christ of God in me, and I radiate this healing, harmonizing, life-giving glory to all humanity. "They that are wise shall shine as the brightness of the firmament; and they that turn many to righteousness as the stars for ever and ever."

Stomach Disorders

I am not impatient, antagonistic, critical, irritable; neither am I anxious or worried. I

trust my Father-God for every need and desire of my life, and I look to Him to make
harmonious my way. All that I eat and all that
I drink are truly from Spirit, and Spirit's peace
and power and harmony pass with my food
into my body—nourishing, upbuilding, and
renewing me in every part. I am temperate,
wise, joyful, and loving, and I continually praise
and give thanks to the Giver of gifts for the
richness with which He supplies the needs of
my mind and body. "I am the living bread
which came down out of heaven: if any man
eat of this bread, he shall live for ever."

Swollen Conditions

I am not puffed up, neither do I entertain
false pride. I am meek and humble in my
Christ likeness. The all-powerful Christ Mind
in me dissolves and dissipates every error accumulation in my mind and body, and every
faculty in me, mental and physical, co-operates
with the indwelling Christ to bring me to perfection. Now am I free, vital, whole; and my
whole being sings in praise to God for His
goodness to me, now and forever. "Blessed are
the meek: for they shall inherit the earth."

Teeth; Treatment for

I do not believe in decay, loss, or limitation of life. The life and substance of Spirit are ever present in me, and I claim their use to make vital and whole and to renew every cell in my teeth. I am sound through and through, lifted up into the consciousness of my oneness with the pure and holy life of my Creator, in whose image and likeness I am continually being renewed. "If ye are led by the Spirit, ye are not under the law."

Tenseness

I am not hurried or worried, for I know that my Redeemer ever liveth to make easy my way. I shift all my loads to the Burden Bearer, who is willing and able to lighten them and who walks always beside me. Now am I open and receptive to the soothing, quieting influence of Spirit, and my whole body becomes supple and relaxed and rested. I am still before Spirit; I find peace with God, and I am renewed and made strong in all my being. "Return unto thy rest, O my soul; / For Jehovah hath dealt bountifully with thee."

Throat: Diphtheria, Tonsillitis

I am not mere flesh and blood subject to inharmony, pain, disease. I am a spiritual being, and I claim the purity of Spirit in my flesh. The breath of God in me cleanses, vitalizes, and heals every cell in my throat, and I am restored to the image and likeness of my Creator—perfect, strong, whole. "All authority hath been given unto me in heaven and on earth," in mind and body, praise God.

Tuberculosis

I am not bound by the beliefs of the race consciousness, neither do I believe in heredity or contagion or infection. I believe in God and His good everywhere present. I give myself fully to the cleansing, vitalizing force of the Spirit of life in me that is mighty to heal. I am eternally one with God, and His breath in me renews every part of my being according to the pattern in the Mount. Now am I strong, courageous, fearless Spirit, and the mind of omniscience in me makes me prosperous and successful in all that I undertake. "As we have borne the image of the earthly, we shall also bear the image of the heavenly."

Tumors

Nothing can find root and nourishment for growth in my mind or body that is not of the Father's planting. I am cleansed through and through by the Lamb of God that taketh away the sins of the world. Every cell in my body is filled with the purifying life and the satisfying substance of Spirit. Everything in me that is foreign to the nature of the Son of God is removed far from me, and I express my perfection in Christ now, praise God! "O Jehovah my God, / I cried unto thee, and thou hast healed me."

Venereal Diseases

I am freed from passion and emotion through the purity of my indwelling Christ. I am lifted up with Christ in God, regenerated in mind and body. The purifying, vitalizing blood of Jesus Christ, shed for me, now flows into every cell of my body, redeeming me from the sins of the flesh. I am regenerated, renewed, harmonized through and through by the life and substance of Spirit, and made a new creature in Christ Jesus, every whit whole.

Weakness

I do not hold weak, vacillating, fearful thoughts in my mind concerning my body or any of the activities of my life. I am one with the Almighty, and His unlimited, inexhaustible strength fills every part of my body. My decisions are strong in wisdom, my body is strong in energy and vigor and life, and I am efficient in all that I do. Spirit holds me and controls me. Spirit guides me and guards me, and I express my divinity now. "God is our refuge and strength, / A very present help in trouble."

Wounds

No wounds or hurts can disturb the life that is within me, for I am one with God-life. Now does the omnipresent life and substance of my Creator fill me and thrill me and heal me, restoring me to His perfection. "I will restore health unto thee, and I will heal thee of thy wounds, saith Jehovah."

ABOUT THE AUTHOR

Though a Kentuckian, Frances W. Foulks claimed universal citizenship because she lived throughout the United States during her life. Coming from a long line of pioneer preachers and religious teachers, she enjoyed continuing their legacy in her chosen field of Christian metaphysics.

Miss Foulks began her career as a businesswoman in the retail and advertising industries but at one point became very ill and found healing through spiritual means. Shortly afterward, she discovered Unity literature, which she began studying and practicing in earnest. On vacation in New York City, she decided to take up a childhood interest, that of needlework designing, which she began to do for magazines and for a large book-publishing firm in New York. There she also found many teachers of metaphysics who deepened her understanding of spiritual Truth.

In 1921, Frances came to Unity School of Christianity for the first time and began an intensive training program. She was ordained in 1923, becoming part of the staff of healing ministers. She became a close friend of Unity cofounder Myrtle Fillmore and later compiled Mrs. Fillmore's correspondence into a book. Also in 1923, she returned to New York for a brief time to study with Emma Curtis Hopkins, the famous New Thought teacher. In 1924, she retired from her staff position at Unity to devote herself full-time to writing, although she continued to be a guest teacher and lecturer at Unity's training school and at other Unity centers.

Rev. Foulks wrote two published books, *All Things Made New* (now out of print) and *Effectual Prayer,* and compiled *Letters of Myrtle Fillmore*, now known as *Myrtle Fillmore's Healing Letters*. She also wrote extensively for all of Unity's periodicals.

Frances W. Foulks made her transition on September 6, 1936. Thanks to her friend Elizabeth Sand Turner, an unpublished work of hers was published in *Unity Magazine* in 1978–79 under the title "Building the Christ Consciousness."

Unity Classic Library Series Offers Timeless Titles of Spiritual Renewal

"Every book in the Unity Classic Library series has earned the "classic" status due to its popularity, durability and uncompromising quality. Each brings a special viewpoint and understanding of Unity's beliefs and principles. The series makes a beautiful display on a library shelf, and each book is a respected addition to any metaphysical collection."

CHARLES FILLMORE

Atom-Smashing Power of Mind

Jesus Christ Heals

Keep a True Lent

Mysteries of Genesis

Mysteries of John

Prosperity

Talks on Truth

CHARLES AND CORA FILLMORE

Teach Us to Pray

The Twelve Powers

LOWELL FILLMORE

The Prayer Way to Health, Wealth, and Happiness

GEORGIANA TREE WEST

Prosperity's Ten Commandments

MYRTLE FILLMORE

How to Let God Help You

H. EMILIE CADY

Lessons in Truth

FRANCES W. FOULKS

Effectual Prayer

IMELDA SHANKLIN

What Are You?

ELIZABETH SAND TURNER

Be Ye Transformed

Let There Be Light

Your Hope of Glory

B0111